THE YOUNG OXFORD BOOK OF

ARCHAEOLOGY

THE YOUNG OXFORD BOOK OF
ARCHAEOLOGY

Norah Moloney

OXFORD UNIVERSITY PRESS

CONTENTS

To my parents with thanks

Oxford University Press

Oxford New York
Athens Auckland Bangkok Bogotá Bombay
Buenos Aires Calcutta Cape Town Dar es Salaam
Delhi Florence Hong Kong Istanbul Karachi
Kuala Lumpur Madras Madrid Melbourne
Mexico City Nairobi Paris Singapore Taipei
Tokyo Toronto Warsaw

and associated companies in
Berlin Ibadan

Copyright © Norah Moloney 1997
Published by Oxford University Press, Inc.
198 Madison Avenue, New York, New York 10016

Originally published by Oxford University Press UK
in 1995

Oxford is a registered trademark of
Oxford University Press

Library of Congress Cataloging-in-Publication Data

Moloney, N. (Norah)
The Young Oxford Book of Archaeology /
Norah Moloney.
p. cm.
Includes index.
1. Archaeology—Juvenile literature. 2. Antiquities—
Juvenile literature. [1. Archaeology. 2. Antiquities.]
I. Title.
C171.M65 1997
930.1—dc21   97-16096
                                  CIP
                                  AC

ISBN 0-19-910067-5 (trade ed.)
ISBN 0-19-521248-7 (lib. ed.)

9 8 7 6 5 4 3 2 1

Printed in Italy by G. Canale & C. S.p.A.
Borgaro T.se - TURIN

1

DECODING THE EVIDENCE

2

A JOURNEY THROUGH TIME

Front cover The Aztec goddess Coatlicue

3

LEARNING FROM THE PAST

INTRODUCTION

From the origins of humankind in Africa almost 4 million years ago humans have spread throughout the entire world. At first they lived in simple shelters eating wild plants and scavenging the remains of dead animals. Gradually they began to gain control over their environment and became expert hunters and farmers. Villages and towns appeared, followed by increasingly complex cities and mighty empires. Today human exploration extends beyond earth into space.

The human success story was made possible by constant changes in technology: tools of stone, wood and bone improved; pottery and metal working were discovered and developed. Technological advances over time have led to the invention of the microchip, the building block of modern technology.

Most of us today are curious about our human past. It is our heritage and we, in turn, contribute to the heritage of generations to come. But past peoples and their activities lie hidden in the shadows of time – shadows which darken the further back in time we go. Who were these people? What did they look like? What did they do? What did they eat? How different were they from us? These are just some of the questions we ask.

In this book you will discover how archaeologists find and interpret the evidence which remains of past peoples, their activities and lifestyles, in order to answer our questions. You will learn, too, about our human journey, which began almost 4 million years ago and which continues today.

Norah Moloney

DECODING THE EVIDENCE

Archaeology is rather like trying to put together a puzzle from which most of the pieces are missing. Archaeological investigation begins with finding a site, and continues long after the digging has finished. The tools of the trade range from simple trowels to highly sophisticated and expensive machines. Using these, archaeologists squeeze the maximum information possible from very scanty evidence.

WHAT IS ARCHAEOLOGY?

Archaeology presents us with breathtaking wonders and gives life to lost heroes and heroines, cities and empires. It also tells us much about everyday life in the past.

For most of us archaeology is linked to mystery and adventure. We associate it with the discovery of the magnificent treasures of the Egyptian Pharaohs and the search for lost cities such as Troy and the Inca mountain settlement of Machu Picchu. Archaeologists are often seen as intrepid adventurers unearthing the glories of the past, bringing to life such heroic figures as Alexander the Great, and revealing the secrets of great empires such as those of Greece and Rome.

Archaeology is also a way of learning about ancient peoples: what they looked like, where they lived, what they ate, what they did, what they believed in, what their customs were. Archaeologists are detectives who attempt to reconstruct past human activities from evidence, for the most part buried beneath the earth.

At one time archaeologists were content to excavate objects so that they could be displayed in museums or private homes. Statues, ceramics and jewellery from countries such as Egypt, Iraq, China and Mexico can be found in museums throughout the world. Today it is not only the objects that are of interest: the location or context in which they are found can tell us a great deal.

Present-day archaeologists are also interested in the way our ancestors lived in, and exploited, their surrounding environment. Just as important is the effect the environment had on their lives. The aim of archaeology today is to discover as complete a picture as possible of life in the past.

Archaeology and history

Isn't archaeology the same as history? Can't we pick up a history book and find out all we want to know about the past? The answer is 'No'. Humankind goes back almost 4 million years. Writing was invented a mere 5000 years ago but was not widespread. Detailed historical records are much more recent than that.

Written history, then, can tell us about only a fraction of our past. We need to study what archaeologists call the 'material remains' of our ancestors if we wish to know about life in the more remote past. Material remains include such things as what is left of houses or other buildings, tools and objects in stone, wood, bone and metal, fragments of pottery, jewellery and

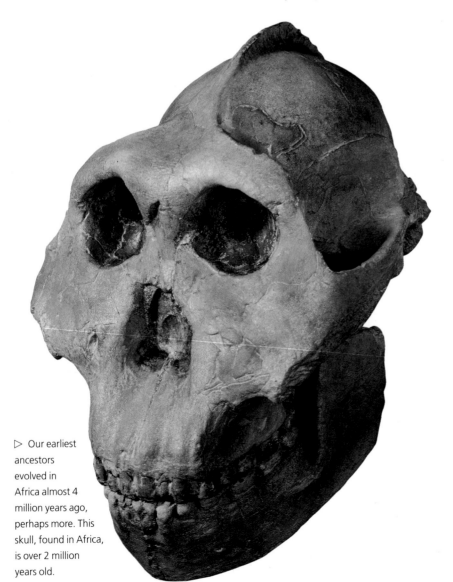

▷ Our earliest ancestors evolved in Africa almost 4 million years ago, perhaps more. This skull, found in Africa, is over 2 million years old.

other adornments, as well as plant and animal remains found on sites.

Why, then, do archaeologists need to excavate remains from more recent periods, which have been recorded by historians, travellers and other interested people? Written history does not deal with everything that happened in the past; it is selective, that is it records specific events such as wars (often only the victories), treaties and coronations, or particular kings and queens and other important people. It may be deliberately distorted, for example to make a person appear more powerful, a victory more glorious, or a place more important. Historical documents usually tell us very little about the everyday life of the ordinary person. They thus give us a partial and unbalanced picture of life in the past. The purpose of archaeology is to supply the information that history leaves out.

▽ Below left: A ram in a tree, made of gold, silver, lapis lazuli, shell and red limestone. It was found in a rich Sumerian grave and dates to about 2500 BC. Below right: The face of a man named Tollund Man, found in a bog in Denmark. He had been strangled, perhaps as part of a ritual, during the 3rd century BC. Bottom left: Machu Picchu in Peru, a 16th-century Inca site located on a mountain peak. Bottom right: Disused railway engines, now part of our industrial past.

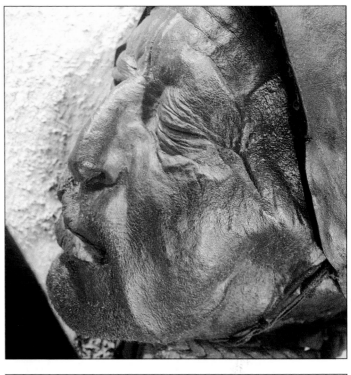

DIFFERENT ARCHAEOLOGIES

Archaeology is used to investigate all periods of time; it looks at everything from the earliest humans to yesterday's rubbish. Prehistoric archaeology deals with the period before the invention of writing, while historic archaeology deals with later periods. Archaeologists specialize in different times within these two large periods. Palaeolithic archaeologists study the period before metals were discovered. Egyptologists specialize in ancient Egypt, while classical archaeologists are interested in ancient Greece and Rome. Industrial archaeologists study evidence of the more recent past relating to areas of activity such as coal mining, railways or old factories.

Environmental archaeology covers all periods. The aim of environmental archaeologists is to reconstruct the past environments in which people, plants and animals lived. Underwater archaeologists explore shipwrecks and waterlogged sites.

In today's expanding world the construction of new buildings sometimes results in archaeological work. For example, builders may uncover archaeological remains as they dig foundations. In these cases archaeologists undertake a rapid excavation of the site to obtain as much information as possible before construction continues. Sometimes an existing archaeological site may need to be protected

before building work can go on. This is known as salvage or rescue archaeology.

Ethnoarchaeologists study the way present-day communities live in order to help them understand the lives of past communities. Experimental archaeologists conduct experiments to discover how things might have been done in the past. This often entails making stone tools or clay pots, building houses or duplicating ancient farming techniques.

Experiments have also been conducted in order to find out what happens to different objects as they lie buried in the ground, and to follow the process of decay over time.

◁ Butser experimental farm in Hampshire, England. For many years archaeologists have conducted experiments here in order to discover how people lived in the Iron Age over 2000 years ago. Archaeologists have reconstructed round houses, granaries and storage pits, grown the same types of crops as were grown at the time, and reared similar animals.

THE EVIDENCE

Our information about the past comes in many forms. First, there are the clearly visible signs: ruined buildings, megalithic stone structures, pyramids. Then there are the objects found in excavations, most commonly fragments or objects made of clay, stone and metal. These are called artefacts because they have been made by humans.

At times, excavation can reveal the plans of individual houses or large buildings. Careful excavation may uncover holes; some of them may have held wooden posts (the wood long since disintegrated), others may have been storage pits or rubbish pits. Patches of earth darkened by burning can indicate ancient fireplaces called hearths. Signs of human activity such as these, which are in context and cannot be moved from a site, are called features.

Sometimes animal bones can be clearly distinguished on sites. Other clues from the past may not be immediately visible: plant remains (burnt or charred grains), pollen grains, soils, and the remains of tiny animals, insects and fish. These, called ecofacts, can tell us much about the diet of our ancestors and the environment in which they lived. The sort of detailed information that specialists can get from some of these artefacts, features and ecofacts is described below.

Pottery

Pottery was invented more than 10,000 years ago. It was easy and cheap to make and could be used for many everyday purposes. Although it breaks easily, pottery rarely disintegrates. As a result fragments of pottery, called sherds, are usually the most common find on all sites younger than 10,000 years old. Because pottery is so abundant, the chapter *The Clay Pots Speak* (pages 142–145) looks at it in detail.

Stone artefacts

Stone is the most durable of all materials, and stone artefacts are sometimes the only evidence of human activity, especially on Palaeolithic sites. Lithic analysts (people who study stone artefacts) get a lot of

information from stone artefacts. They can often determine where the stone came from, how the artefact was made, and what it was used for. Geologists help archaeologists locate the source of stone, which may have been collected close to the site or at some distance from it.

Some archaeologists attempt to manufacture stone tools and larger stone objects in order to gain an understanding of the range of techniques needed to work stone;

△ Fragments of pottery are the most common find on most sites, except the earliest. Whole pots occur more rarely. The way pottery has been made, the patterns on pots, and their shapes can reveal much about the people who made them.

▽ Before the invention of pottery, our ancestors made their implements from stone, bone and wood. Stone is hardwearing and rarely disintegrates. As a result it is often only stone artefacts that are found on very old sites.

some stone artefacts are more difficult, require more skill and take more time to make than others. At times it is possible to fit pieces of stone together, rather like a jigsaw puzzle. This is called refitting and can show us how the tool maker used the stone to make the tool.

Refitting can also show if the artefact was made or used in one place or in different areas of the site. This kind of experimental and refitting work has even enabled archaeologists to distinguish between the best stoneworkers in a community and the apprentices.

Microscopic studies of stone tools reveal what the tools were used for. Such studies can show that a particular tool was used to saw wood or cut meat, for example. At times minute fragments or residues of the material on which the tool was used can be recognized (animal hairs or fat, for example). Microscopic traces of blood have been recognized on tools which are 90,000 years old.

It is also possible to see the damage to the stones, called hammer stones, that were used to batter, pound or break other stones.

Animal bones

These are often the best indicators of ancient people's diet. Faunal analysts (those who study animal remains) can determine the type of bone, the age, sex and size of the animal it came from, and whether the animal was killed by humans

△ Excavations of the hill-fort of Maiden Castle in England revealed this iron arrowhead in the spine of the soldier it had killed almost 2000 years ago.

or carnivorous animals or died of natural causes. Once the animal has been identified, its age may be estimated from the size and appearance of the bones. Age can be judged most accurately from the number of teeth (fewer in younger animals) and the wear on teeth. The teeth of older animals are more worn down than those of younger animals.

The number and sex of each animal found may provide information on hunting and rearing strategies. If domestic animals (farm animals) were kept for meat, for example, the young would usually have been killed because of their tender meat. However, a few older animals might have been kept for breeding purposes. Most bones on the site will therefore be those of young animals. If animals were kept primarily for

their milk, the bones on a site may be predominantly those of the adult females who provided the milk.

Animals generally give birth at a particular time of the year. It is therefore possible to work out the season a site was occupied by calculating the age of the younger animals.

Animal bones can indicate the type of environment around the site. Some animals (such as deer, bear and wolf) prefer woodland, while others (elephant, horse and mammoth) prefer grasslands. Many animals are adapted to particular climates: mammoth and reindeer, for example, are cold climate species, while the presence of rhinos and giraffes indicate warmer climates.

Faunal analysts are able to distinguish between the bones of wild and domesticated animals. This helps the archaeologists track the slow transition from hunting to settled farming which happened about 10,000 years ago. Wild and domesticated animals may have been used not only as food but also as a source of clothing, fuel and bones for tool manufacture.

Insects, snails and fish

Although insects and snails may seem insignificant, they can be of great value to the archaeologist as most species live in special habitats and are sensitive to changes in climate. Their remains (usually

◁ A shell midden from Los Roques in Venezuela. Shell middens are mounds of shells from shellfish which once provided food for groups of people living in coastal areas. By studying these shells, archaeologists can discover important information on diet, collecting techniques, and the season when sites were occupied.

only snails' shells and the hard parts of beetles' bodies) thus provide information about the climate and environment at the time the site was occupied.

Fish bones, too, can tell us much, although individual species are very difficult to distinguish. Some fish shoal (gather together) at particular times of the year, so fish bones can help us to discover at what season coastal sites were occupied. Fish remains may also provide us with information on ancient fishing methods. Shell middens, huge mounds of discarded shells from shellfish, are a feature of many coastal areas. These are valuable sources of information on ancient diet as well as the season when sites were occupied.

Human remains

As with animal bones, it is possible to tell whether human bones belong to young or old, males or females. Male bones are usually larger than female ones, and some, in particular the pelvis, are a different shape.

By the time we stop growing, the ends of the long bones in our arms and legs have fused together. Archaeologists look for signs of fusion to determine if bones are from a child or an adult.

Bones become deformed by certain diseases. A specialist can distinguish which disease affected the bone. We may also find injuries caused by weapons. If the bones had healed we know that the injury was not fatal, whereas unhealed bones indicate that the person died a violent death.

It is even possible to determine the type of weapon used from the shape of the mark left on the bone, and sometimes to tell the direction of the fatal blow.

Much more information can be obtained from bones. Periods of malnutrition suffered by children can be detected in their bones and teeth. Wear on bone can indicate that people did particular types of work, such as carrying heavy loads on the back. It is even possible to see early attempts at surgery.

△ Human bones can tell us a great deal. The distortion in the tibia (lower legbone) here shows a fracture which has healed. The bone would have been much shorter as a result, so the person would have limped badly.

▽ Evidence of a fatal sword wound to the skull of a soldier during a battle against the Romans in England. The neatness of the cut at the top of the wound shows that the sword blow was struck from above.

▷ This person would have suffered greatly with toothache. The outer enamel has worn off the teeth, exposing the inner yellow dentine. Caries (decay) have destroyed part of the lower molar (second from right), which also has an abscess. A second abscess hole can be seen by another tooth.

Human teeth

Teeth, too, hold a wealth of information for those who know how to decipher it. They are important indicators of age. Milk teeth belong to children. Teeth which are very worn down probably come from older people, although worn teeth can also indicate a diet of gritty food. Some people used their teeth to hold materials, such as leather, leaving both arms free to work the material. Years of this kind of work leaves particular, recognizable marks on teeth. As with bones, we can see from teeth and jaws if a person suffered from tooth decay, gum disease or abscesses.

◁ The dryness of the Egyptian climate helped preserve many types of food in dried form. The food here, which comes from Egyptian tombs, includes pieces of duck, loaves of bread, a plate of figs and some fish.

△ Charred (partly burnt) seeds of emmer, an early form of wheat. These come from a granary in Mycenae (ancient Greece), which was burnt in a raid about 1100 BC.

Plant remains

Plants do not survive as easily as bones. The fact that we find fewer remains on sites does not mean that plants were not eaten and used. Sometimes cereal grains and fruits have survived in charred form, if they were cooked or heated by fire. We often find evidence for the use of plants even though we may not find the plants themselves.

Utensils, such as mortars and pestles, which were used to prepare plant food, are common finds on sites. Pots are sometimes decorated with illustrations of plants. The shapes of grains have also been found impressed in clay pots.

Archaeobotanists can distinguish between wild plants and those which have been specially grown by humans (domesticated plants). In this way we learn how ancient populations gradually began to grow their own crops and how they continued to use wild plants to supplement their own produce.

Pollen

All flowering plants have pollen. Pollen grains are made of silica; they are very sturdy and not easily destroyed. The grain shape is specific to the plant. Specialists who look at pollen grains through a microscope are often able to tell which plant the pollen belongs to. Because many plants grow only in a particular environment, pollen provides clues about that environment at different points in time. As a result pollen can provide a picture of changes in the vegetation of the surrounding landscape, perhaps from woodland to shrub or grassland, or the reverse. Such changes may be due to the climate or human action. Fluctuations in pollen can be shown on a diagram, which then provides a clear picture of the changing landscape in which our ancestors lived. Such sequences have been particularly useful to show the changing environment in northern Europe over the last 10,000 years.

These are just a few examples of the types of evidence which form part of modern-day archaeological research.

Other lines of study include soil analysis, study of land formation, analysis of metal objects, and the analysis of coprolites, the fossilized faeces of animals and humans.

How the evidence survives

The evidence of past lives that we find on archaeological sites is generally just a fraction of what was once there. Most has disintegrated or been lost. Many factors affect the preservation of archaeological sites: the climate, the type of soil, the speed at which objects are buried, and the extent to which they are disturbed after burial. Through the ages villages, towns and cities have been built and expanded, and the land has been greatly altered by farming and by the building of roads and railways. Such large-scale development of the landscape has destroyed or hidden much evidence of the past.

Preservation also depends on the chemical and physical properties of the objects: organic materials such as bone, plants, food, hair, wood and leather are much more likely to disintegrate than inorganic ones such as stone, clay and metals.

GOOD AND BAD CONDITIONS FOR PRESERVATION

Organic materials require special conditions of burial in order to survive. These delicate materials have been found in arid, frozen or waterlogged environments. Wooden artefacts, textiles, flowers, baskets and food have been preserved in Egypt, coastal Peru and central Asia because the hot, dry climate prevents decay. In these places bodies several thousand years old have been found which still have skin, hair and nails; they have been naturally mummified by the arid climate.

Extremely cold conditions are also excellent for preserving delicate materials. It is rather like keeping them in a freezer. Mammoth remains have been found in the frozen soils of Siberia and fully clothed human bodies, hundreds of years old, have been found in Greenland and Alaska.

Objects can be preserved in the wet and airless environment of lakes and bogs. There have been spectacular discoveries of fully preserved bodies buried over 2000 years ago in peat bogs in England, Ireland and Denmark. A 6000-year-old wooden trackway was preserved beneath a peat bog in

⊲ Trees, plants and shrubs grow extremely rapidly in tropical climates. The jungle has almost completely hidden the unexcavated part of the Mayan site of Kabah in the Yucatan peninsula of Mexico. The first explorers to discover Mayan sites had to hack their way through jungle growth such as this.

England, while the remains of lakeside villages with wooden houses have been found in some Swiss lakes.

Tropical climates are disastrous for preservation. Rainforests grow rapidly and can hide buildings within a year. Current excavators of ancient Mayan sites in the tropical forests of Central America have to cut away a year's growth of vegetation before they begin each new season of excavation. In such environments tree roots affect the foundations of buildings, often causing them to break up and collapse. Finding sites in such situations is extremely difficult.

Soils affect preservation. Acid soils quickly destroy bone and wood. However, a slight change in the colour of the soil at a particular place can indicate the former presence of organic substances. This is how archaeologists recognize holes where wooden posts once stood and the foundations of wooden huts. Luckily, not all soils are destructive: bone, for example, keeps well in chalky soils.

Occasionally disasters occur which seal sites and preserve them almost completely. The volcanic eruption of Vesuvius in AD 79 preserved the Roman cities of Pompeii and Herculaneum in Italy. Boats that were sunk in storms and battles often have an almost complete cargo. These special conditions of preservation provide a vast amount of information for the archaeologist.

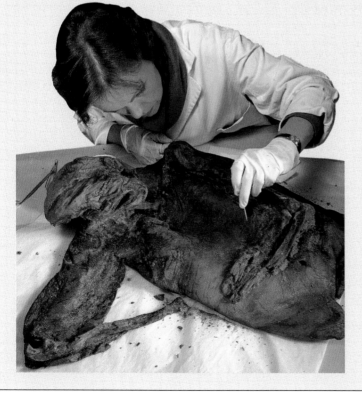

⊲ The body of a 25-year-old man, known as Lindow Man, was found in a bog in England. He had lain there for almost 2000 years, his body preserved by the wet and oxygen-free (anaerobic) conditions. He had been knocked out by two blows to the head, strangled, and had his throat cut, in what may have been a ritual sacrifice.

LOCATING SITES

How do we find archaeological sites? Some sites have never been lost to us. The Egyptian pyramids, megalithic monuments such as Stonehenge, and some Greek and Roman buildings have been visible to generations of people since they were built.

However, detective work is required to find most sites. This can begin at home or in the library. The archaeologist looks for old place names on early maps or places mentioned in old texts such as the Bible. Often myths and legends such as those of the Greeks and Vikings document past events and places, giving clues to their location. This is how both ancient Troy and the Viking settlement in Canada were discovered. Sometimes archaeologists get vital information or clues by talking to local people who can direct them to sites.

◁ Surface survey, or fieldwalking, in Veneto, Italy. Fieldwalking is most useful after fields have been ploughed, as ploughing may bring objects to the surface such as pottery sherds and stone artefacts. Sites are most commonly found through field-walking – often a tedious and back-breaking job.

Survey

Careful study of land surfaces on geological maps often helps to pinpoint areas which may have been good for settlement and where favourable conditions for preservation exist. Fertile soils are good for farming; water is vital, so places close to ponds, wells and rivers could have attracted early settlers. Areas rich in raw materials such as stone, clay, metal ores and precious stones may also have attracted people. Once likely areas have been identified, the next step is to survey

them by walking over the area, scanning the ground for any artefacts which may have found their way to the surface. Usually the area is divided into sections so that a systematic surface survey can be done. In promising locations – perhaps where a collection of artefacts has been found on the surface – a small test excavation is undertaken to see what lies beneath the ground. A larger excavation may then take place if a site is located.

Aerial photography

Traces of sites are sometimes visible only from the air. The growth of crops forms a slightly different pattern over buried sites from that over the surrounding area. The soil is richer over pits and ditches, so crops growing over these will be taller and thicker than others around. However, the soil is not as rich over buried walls and

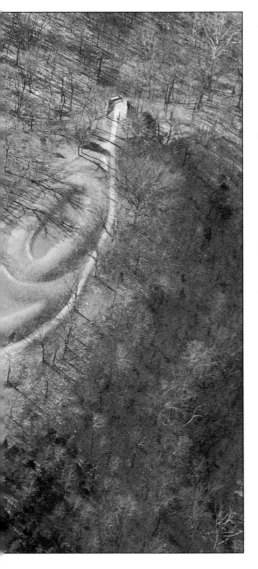

◁ Great Serpent Mound in Ohio, USA, built between about 500 and 100 BC and used for ceremonial occasions. It is in the form of a serpent, clearly visible from the air, and is almost 390 m long, 6 m wide and 1.5 m high.

△ A landscape affected by erosion in the Hadar region of Ethiopia. The earliest sites in East Africa have been exposed through erosion. Archaeologists survey recently exposed surfaces in search of early hominid sites.

crops do not grow as well. These differences create patterns which can be detected from the air. Photographs that have been taken from satellites can show the extent of large-scale features such as irrigation canals and roads. Once a site has been located by aerial photography, archaeologists can then proceed with surface survey.

Subsurface detection

Today many sophisticated techniques are used to detect objects and features beneath the surface. Perhaps the best known is the common metal detector. However, there are more advanced magnetic instruments which can detect slight traces of iron in the soil. Other instruments measure electrical waves which pass through the soil from buried sites.

Subsurface detection devices such as these allow archaeologists to get as much information as possible about a site without having to disturb the surface. It is then much easier for them to pinpoint the best places for excavation.

Natural causes

Many of the oldest sites lie beneath hundreds of metres of earth. Movement of the land, such as earthquakes, may bring them to the surface. Over hundreds of thousands of years winds, rains and the hot sun cause the land surface to erode. Natural erosion can often reveal deeply buried sites. Most of the very early hominid sites in East Africa and Java were discovered by surface survey in areas affected by erosion and earthquake activity.

Accidental discovery

Sometimes artefacts and sites are discovered accidentally. A farmer ploughing his fields in England uncovered a hoard of silver and gold jewellery which had been buried for over 2000 years. Workers digging a ditch for electricity cables beneath Mexico City uncovered part of the Great Temple of the Aztecs. Construction work in cities and on new roadways may reveal evidence of the past. Indeed, while modern development disturbs sites it can also reveal many which would otherwise have been lost to us.

STRATIGRAPHY

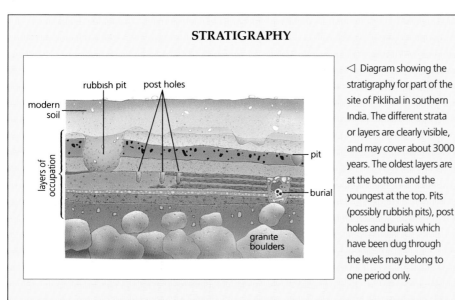

rubbish pit   post holes

modern soil

layers of occupation

pit

burial

granite boulders

◁ Diagram showing the stratigraphy for part of the site of Piklihal in southern India. The different strata or layers are clearly visible, and may cover about 3000 years. The oldest layers are at the bottom and the youngest at the top. Pits (possibly rubbish pits), post holes and burials which have been dug through the levels may belong to one period only.

Why are most archaeological sites buried beneath the ground? There are a number of ways in which this can happen. Abandoned sites are gradually covered by weeds, grasses and earth. Abandoned buildings will eventually collapse and may also be covered by vegetation and earth. Sometimes other buildings are constructed on top of the remains of earlier ones. Sites may be covered by sand, wind-blown soil or flood deposits. Natural catastrophes such as earthquakes or volcanic eruptions can bury sites. Over thousands of years a site may become more deeply buried as it is covered by layers of sand, soil or other buildings.

This series of strata, or changing layers of deposits, is known in archaeological terms as stratigraphy. Each layer of deposits, or stratum, relates to one period of time when a site was occupied. It is important in excavation to understand the stratigraphy of a site, especially those sites which have been used frequently by different groups, in order to be certain which layer the archaeological materials belong to. Various factors can cause stratigraphic layers and the artefacts they contain to become mixed up, for example burrowing animals, a rubbish pit dug from one layer which goes through another layer, and movements of the earth.

EXCAVATION

There are two principal ways of excavating a site. The first consists of removing the layers of the site one at a time. This enables the archaeologist to discover what happened at one particular period in time. Horizontal excavation thus gives us a slice of time and allows the archaeologist to look at the connections between artefacts, ecofacts and features. It is a good method to use for sites which have been occupied perhaps once or twice, such as Palaeolithic hunting camps. It is also useful if we want to see the layout of a village.

Other sites may have been used time and time again so that there are successive layers of occupation. The Near East is dotted with huge mounds, or tells, which have grown in size over time as people built houses and towns on the remains of earlier, ruined buildings. Here archaeologists may excavate downwards through the mound by digging trenches in a few areas in order to get a picture of the activities which occurred over a long period of time. Vertical excavation thus slices through time, enabling the archaeologist to see changes which may have occurred from one period to another.

In very deep sites it is too dangerous to excavate vertically from the top to the bottom. The sides of the trench could collapse as the excavation goes deeper. In such cases an area is opened on the surface and the excavation continues downwards

◁ Excavations in progress in the Hadar region of Ethiopia, where many early human fossils have been found. This illustration shows different aspects of excavation. Two men record the position of an object and another carries a bucket of soil to be passed through a sieve. Two more men search for fossils in the soil and gravel remaining after sieving.

◁ The site of El Aculadero in southern Spain. Some of the many activities that occur during excavation can be seen in this photo of excavators working in their well-defined square. Activities include excavation, recording, putting artefacts into bags, cleaning a square and sweeping the soil into a small pan. The soil in the large pan will be passed through a sieve.

in a sloping series of steps. This type of excavation is called step trenching.

Sometimes both vertical and horizontal methods of excavation are used on one site, but rarely is a site excavated totally. It is too expensive. It is also vital to leave something for future excavations when techniques may have improved or archaeologists may have different problems to solve.

Starting an excavation

At the start of an excavation a datum point is set. This is a clearly visible spot or object which is used as a fixed reference for measuring the exact vertical and horizontal location of everything on the site. A plan of the surface of the site is then made.

The excavation area is usually divided into one-metre squares, which can be further divided into smaller squares. Each large square is given a number or letter. This helps the excavators, or diggers as they are more commonly called, to plot the exact position of a find on a map.

When they begin an excavation archaeologists remove the topsoil or overburden, the most recent layer covering the site; they use shovels, or a machine if the topsoil is very deep. When the

▷ Fine brushes or dental probes are used to excavate objects that are likely to break or disintegrate. Here the excavator carefully removes soil particles surrounding a fossil during excavation of an early human site at Laetoli, Tanzania. The work requires precision and great concentration to reveal the fossil successfully.

archaeological layer is exposed, diggers carefully scrape away the soil with trowels and excavate delicate objects with dental probes or similar instruments. The soil is brushed into a small dustpan and put in a bucket. From time to time the digger stops excavating and makes a plan of the square, recording all that has been revealed.

Recording the finds

At the same time as excavation reveals the past, it destroys the site. It is therefore vital to keep detailed records of everything that happens on a site: the way it is excavated, the position of the artefacts and ecofacts, the position and type of features, changes in soil colour and problems which occur. Detailed plans and photographs must record every step of the excavation.

It is vital to record the exact position of each object and feature in relation to the square it is in and to relate it to the datum point. In this way the vertical and horizontal location of all finds can be determined.

While excavation reveals evidence which can be kept such as artefacts, and human, animal and plant remains, it destroys data such as features. If all data are recorded and the exact position of everything is plotted on a plan, the archaeologist has a map of each layer as it is excavated. The site photographer takes many photographs of each layer, which can be checked against the plan. All

photographs have a small measuring scale to indicate size. These plans and photographs show the position of features, artefacts and ecofacts on a site and how they may be associated with each other. A dark patch of earth surrounded by animal bones, for example, could be the remains of a meal around a fireplace; a series of small round holes may be the post holes of a hut. When they are back at the laboratory archaeologists use the plans and photographs to help them reconstruct a picture of the different layers of the site.

Diggers sometimes have specially prepared recording sheets on which they fill out the details of their finds. These data are later entered into a computer. Today computers are increasingly used to record and produce plans of excavations, so saving a great deal of time.

Sieving the soil

The soil which is swept up during excavation is taken away and sieved to check for any small bones or artefacts that may have been missed in the excavation. Sometimes the soil is passed through one sieve, sometimes it passes through a number of increasingly smaller and finer sieves. In this way the smallest objects, such as rodent bones or teeth, are found.

Sieves can also be placed in water and shaken. This causes the soil to dissolve and fall through the sieve but it captures the objects. As the water washes everything,

△ Recording the evidence. To help her make an accurate plan, the excavator uses a squared drawing frame and a lead attached to string to indicate the position of objects.

▽ The soil removed during excavation is passed through a sieve to catch remains missed by the excavator. Other people check the soil in pans for larger remains.

SPECIALISTS

Today many different people take part in excavations and in post-excavation studies. There are specialists in stone artefacts, pottery, metal artefacts, bones and plant remains. In addition there may be soil analysts, geologists and people who specialize in dating techniques. While it is easy to input data on computers, specialists may also be needed for the mathematical and statistical programmes which are used to look for patterns in the data. Then there are the photographers and the artists who photograph and draw the artefacts. These are just a few of the many different people who are involved in archaeology.

bones can be easily distinguished from stones. Seeds and other organic remains can be recovered through a process known as water flotation. In this process tiny remains float to the surface of the water while the heavier soil sinks and flows away.

Processing the finds

What happens to the artefacts and ecofacts uncovered during the excavation? Once their position has been mapped and the objects fully recorded, they are taken to the site laboratory. Here they are cleaned and clearly labelled with a code showing the level and square they came from. They are then sorted into different groups, for example pottery, stone tools and bones. The finds are carefully wrapped and placed in bags for transfer to off-site laboratories, usually at the institutions involved in the excavation.

Archaeologists on the site also collect samples of other materials such as charcoal and soil. Special analysis of charcoal can provide dates for the site (see pages 26–27). Soil samples are useful to check the type of soil surrounding the site; they are also likely to contain organic material such

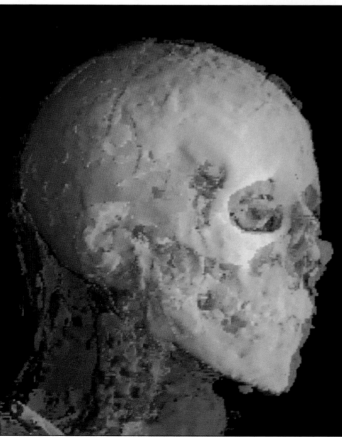

△ Workers in the laboratory search through the many thousands of pottery sherds, found during an excavation, to reconstruct pots. It is a massive jigsaw puzzle.

◁ Archaeology and modern science. This three-dimensional image of the skull of an Egyptian mummy was made by a scanning machine. This enables archaeologists to study the mummy without unwrapping and destroying it.

as pollen, seeds and insect remains.

Fragile objects may require special treatment by a conservator at the site. Pieces which are in danger of falling apart can be strengthened with special glue, just strong enough to allow the objects to be taken safely back to the main laboratory. Particularly delicate pieces may be protected by covering them with plaster of Paris, polyurethane foam or latex rubber before they are transported.

Publishing the results

Each specialist involved in the excavation writes a report on what he or she has studied. These reports are put together to form the site report, which is then published either as a book or in special archaeological or scientific journals. In addition, shorter articles describing particular aspects of the site are often published. It is necessary for archaeologists to let others know the results of their studies as quickly as possible. This helps us to learn about and understand more fully what happened in the past.

WHEN DID IT HAPPEN?

Reconstruction of past activities is incomplete unless we can place them at a specific point in time. 'How old is it?' is one of the fundamental questions in archaeology.

▷ This superbly crafted flint tool comes from the later part of the Palaeolithic or Stone Age, known as the Upper Palaeolithic; it is between 19,000 and 17,000 years old. It is called a Solutrean laurel leaf: 'Solutrean' after the site of Solutré in France where this tool type was first found and 'laurel leaf' because of its shape. Archaeologists have demonstrated that it can take up to eight hours to make such a tool.

◁ An Iron Age spearhead decorated in bronze found in the River Thames in southern England. The Iron Age in southern England lasted from about 600 BC to AD 43, the year the Roman army invaded England.

It was widely believed in Europe before the 19th century that the world had begun in the year 4004 BC and was therefore less than 6000 years old. This calculation was based on the dates of events narrated in the Bible. During the 19th century the study of fossils, the development of geology and the discovery of stone tools and the bones of extinct animals along the sides of European river valleys made people review their ideas. These remains were surely more than 6000 years old.

RELATIVE DATING

Archaeologists use many different methods to determine if one artefact is older or younger than another. These methods, which are known as relative dating, do not provide exact dates, but they are successfully used by archaeologists to place artefacts in their correct chronological order.

The Three Age System

In the early 19th century an exhibition of prehistoric artefacts was held in the Danish National Museum. Christian J. Thomsen, curator of the museum, prepared the exhibits according to the material they were made of: stone, bronze and iron. He discovered that the tools that were found in the oldest layers of the river valleys were always made of stone. In later levels these were replaced by bronze tools, which were in turn replaced by iron tools.

It was clear that most stone tools were older than bronze tools, and that these were in turn older than iron tools. Thomsen called the period in which only stone tools were used the Stone Age. He named the period in which bronze tools were used the Bronze Age, and the following period the Iron Age. This is known as the Three Age System and the terms continue to be employed in archaeology today, although each has been further subdivided. The Stone Age, for example, has been divided into three parts: the Palaeolithic (Old Stone Age), the Mesolithic (Middle Stone Age) and the Neolithic (New Stone Age).

△ Tell Nebi Mend, Syria. People have built their houses in the same place for over 8000 years. As a result an artificial hill has formed, and the houses of the people who live there today are built on the remains of thousands of years of human occupation.

◁ Bronze ritual vessel from China's Shang civilization (16th to 11th centuries BC). Master metal workers, the Shang produced fine bronzes. This vessel, in the form of a tiger protecting a man, is beautifully decorated with feline and serpent designs.

Stratigraphic time

Stratigraphy (the separate layers or strata of deposits which accumulate over time) has been used since the 19th century as an aid to discovering if one object, or archaeological level, is older or younger than another. Each layer of deposits, or stratum, is younger than the stratum on which it lies. Put another way, the lower stratum is older than the upper one. We can then say that anything, including archaeological material, in one stratum is older or younger than that in another stratum. However, we do not know how much older or younger as the period of time each layer takes to form varies according to conditions. For example, a deep layer of sand may have been deposited in a very short time owing to a sand storm, whereas other deposits may have taken millennia – thousands of years – to form. The position of artefacts in stratigraphic sequences (layers) was used to confirm the differences between the Stone, Bronze and Iron Ages. Some sites have very long stratigraphic sequences, with many occupation layers which may cover many centuries.

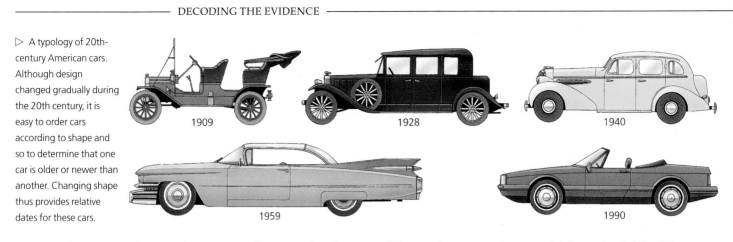

▷ A typology of 20th-century American cars. Although design changed gradually during the 20th century, it is easy to order cars according to shape and so to determine that one car is older or newer than another. Changing shape thus provides relative dates for these cars.

1909   1928   1940   1959   1990

Ordering with typology

If we look at objects from the 20th century, cars or clothes for example, we can easily see how they have changed from the beginning of the century to the present day. We can place them in order fairly accurately, from the oldest to the most recent, based on changes in their size, shape, decoration and so on. In this way we separate the old-fashioned from the modern. When we do this we are creating what is called in archaeological terms a typology.

Archaeologists use typologies not only to organize artefacts but also to help them get relative dates for objects. They sort the objects from an excavation into large groups of stone, bone, bronze and ceramics, for instance. They then sort each of these into smaller groups which have some aspect in common such as shape, decoration or manner of manufacture. By carefully checking the stratigraphic position of the artefacts, archaeologists have been able to determine that changes in pattern or type of artefact are associated with different time periods.

Typologies have been developed for all kinds of artefacts including stone, bronze and iron tools, bronze and iron weapons, and ceramic pots. Archaeological artefacts are often dated to a particular period by comparing them with artefacts already known to belong to that period. While typology is useful in providing a relative date, it should be confirmed by some other dating method.

Animals and biostratigraphy

Biostratigraphic dating is based on fossilized animal remains found in a stratigraphic sequence. Modern animals have evolved over millions of years. Changes occurring in some, such as pigs, horses and elephants, are distinctive and specialists have been able to form a family tree or sequence of change for these animals. Pigs' molar teeth, for example, changed often and rapidly. When they are found in a deposit we know that the deposit itself is probably at least as old as the fossil teeth in it. This form of relative dating is particularly useful for the early Palaeolithic period.

Pollen dating

Plants and trees produce sturdy pollen grains, which are usually well preserved in bogs and lakes. To study these, a pollen analyst inserts a large tube, called a core, into the waterlogged deposit. When removed it is filled with a column of sediments which come from all depths of the lake or bog. The analyst then studies the core to see what pollen is present at various levels. Sometimes a sequence of different pollen types, indicating a succession of changes in the environment, can be constructed. Pollen from a site in the area can then be compared with the sequence and a relative date for the site obtained.

Deep sea cores

Sediments have been slowly accumulating on the ocean bed. These sediments contain the shells of microscopic marine organisms called foraminifera. Analysts take samples of sediments from the sea bed with a special machine which drills a core through the ocean sediments. As with pollen cores, deep sea cores show changes in climate, because foraminifera are very sensitive to climatic change. We now have an accurate sequence of temperature changes which goes back 2.3 million years. This gives a relative date for particular climatic changes such as glacial and interglacial periods.

ABSOLUTE DATING

Relative dating methods can give us some indication of the chronological position of a site or an object. Archaeologists like to use different relative dating techniques to be sure of getting an approximate age. They use other, mainly scientific methods to get true or absolute dates; these allow us to determine the age of a site with much greater precision. Whenever possible, absolute dating techniques are used to verify relative dates for a site and vice versa.

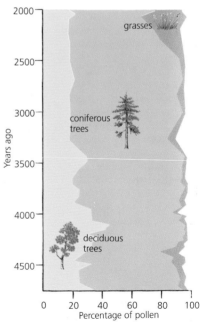

△ Pollen diagram showing an area dominated by coniferous forest for almost 3000 years. At times other types of vegetation increase, indicating changes in climate or forest clearances, possibly for farmland.

CALENDARS AND HISTORICAL DATES

Before the development of scientific dating methods, people relied on chronologies of events recorded by historians, or calendars used by ancient peoples. Recording in ancient times differed from country to country. Sometimes an event was given a date based on the accession to the throne of a particular king. Many lists of kings and dynasties have been found, particularly in ancient Egypt, Mesopotamia and China. Unfortunately the dates on such lists may not be completely accurate, especially as we go further back in time. Today, however, archaeologists are able to correlate these ancient dates with our own calendar.

Some ancient civilizations had their own calendars. Such calendars can be deciphered and correlated with ours, and so provide absolute dates for objects which have dates under an ancient system. The Mayan calendar, for example, consisted of an intricate system of numbers and glyphs or signs representing the days and months. Its starting point is 11 August 3114 BC, according to our calendar. Archaeologists studying Mayan civilization can use the deciphered calendars to date sites with great accuracy.

▷ Part of a Mayan calendar from Menché, Mexico. The Maya used two calendars. The 365-day solar or farmer's calendar was divided into 18 months of 20 days. There were five extra days which were thought to be unlucky. Each day was represented by a glyph (sign). A second calendar was used for religious purposes and astrology. It had a 260-day cycle with 20 weeks each consisting of 13 numbered days. The two calendars ended together once every 52 years, a time feared by the people.

Tree ring dating

Tree ring dating, or dendrochronology, has been used to obtain absolute dates since the 17th century. Each year leaves its mark on a tree in the form of a growth ring of new wood; we can see and count these when the tree is cut down. As growth is affected by climate, rings are not always the same thickness; they are usually wider after a good growing season and narrower after a poor season. Furthermore, rings get thinner as the tree gets older. Growth rings of the same year can be identified on trees of the same species. By comparing and linking patterns of tree rings, a sequence of overlapping patterns can be built up. Such sequences may cover thousands of years in some areas.

This type of dating is used in regions where particular trees continue growing for long periods and conditions are good for preserving wood. The sequence of tree rings for the bristlecone pine in California, in the United States, for example, extends back 8000 years.

Radioactive dating

This method of dating is based on naturally occurring radioactive elements in different types of material. Scientists have discovered that certain of these radioactive elements decay or disappear at a constant rate over time. This rate of decay can be calculated accurately. However, the radioactive elements which decay are not the same in all objects. Different methods need to be used depending on the type of object to be dated. Some techniques can be applied to organic objects (bone, charcoal, wood), some are used on volcanic rock, and others are used with pottery. Carbon 14, potassium-argon and thermoluminescence are all methods of radioactive dating.

Carbon 14

Carbon 14 (written C-14) is one of the most useful dating methods in archaeology. It is used to date charcoal, wood, bones, plants and shells. All living things – people,

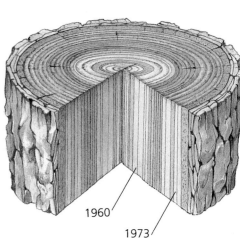

1960

1973

△ Trees produce annual growth rings of varying widths which can be counted. The yearly rings are similar in trees of the same species. Consequently a sequence of overlapping ring patterns can be formed and a date for the wood sample can be determined.

◁ The annual growth rings from a section of an elm tree are clearly visible. When it can be used, tree ring dating is the most accurate of absolute dating methods.

carbon 14

wood used for fire/ cooking

◁ Carbon 14 (C-14) dating. The amount of radioactive carbon present in an archaeological sample is determined using a machine called a mass spectrometer. An age for the sample is then worked out.

△ Plants absorb C-14 from the atmosphere. It is passed to animals and humans in the food chain. It is also in wood used for fires. At death C-14 begins to decay. As we know its rate of decay, we can calculate the age of an object.

animals and plants – contain a certain amount of radioactive carbon, called carbon 14. C-14 is produced in the atmosphere and absorbed by plants. It is passed on to animals and humans in the food chain. On death this carbon begins to decay or disappear. Scientists have been able to calculate the rate at which it decays: after 5730 years half the original carbon disappears, after a further 5730 years another half of the remaining carbon decays, and so on. Age can be calculated by measuring the amount of C-14 in the archaeological object and working backwards from today. Archaeologists can use C-14 to calculate the dates of objects up to 40,000 or even 50,000 years old. By then most of the radioactive element in the object has disappeared, so C-14 cannot be used to ascertain the age of objects which are more than 50,000 years old.

Potassium-argon

Like C-14, potassium-argon (written as K-Ar) is a dating method based on the known rate of decay of a radioactive element. In the case of K-Ar, an isotope of potassium decays into argon gas in volcanic rocks. The rate of decay is extremely slow: it takes about 1.3 billion

years for half of the original radioactive isotope to decay. This method dates the formation of the rocks and can be used on rocks which are more than 100,000 years old. It has been especially useful in providing dates for the oldest sites in Africa and elsewhere, which, luckily for us, were set in a volcanic landscape. K-Ar does not date the object but the context in which the object lies. Many African sites, for example, lie sandwiched between two layers of volcanic sediment called volcanic

tuffs. As the tuffs can be dated, we know that the age of the site lies between the age of the upper and lower tuffs.

Thermoluminescence

On most sites from the Neolithic onwards, sherds of pottery usually far outnumber all other artefacts. Pottery contains radioactive elements which accumulate at a known rate through time. When heated to 500° C or more, the electrons of the radioactive element escape in the form of light energy called thermoluminescence (written as TL). When a pottery object was originally fired to harden it, all the TL present in the clay mixture would have been released, and the radioactive clock would have been reset at zero. The process of trapping TL electrons would then have begun once more. To calculate the date at which a pot was fired, the TL specialist reheats a sample of the pot to release the TL accumulated since the original firing. The TL can then be measured and converted into an age measurement. TL dating can also be used on burnt flints.

TL dating is suitable for objects up to 80,000 years old. It can thus be applied to burnt flints from the Palaeolithic which extend beyond the C-14 limit of 50,000 years.

Although scientific research continues to develop dating techniques which allow us to date a variety of objects with accuracy, there remain some objects which cannot be dated accurately (for example unburnt flint tools). Nevertheless, archaeologists are increasingly able to answer the question, 'How old is it?'

WRITING ARCHAEOLOGICAL DATES

Many more methods have been developed to provide absolute dates for archaeological objects and sites. We must, however, be able to write the dates in a way that can be understood by everyone. Three terms are used in archaeology: BC, AD and BP. These are based on two fixed points in time from which years can be counted forwards or backwards. The first point is the birth of Christ and is known as the year AD 1 (AD means *Anno Domini*, the Latin for 'In the Year of Our Lord'). We count years backwards from AD 1 for events before Christ (BC) and forwards

from AD 1 for events after. For example, 360 BC means 360 years before the year AD 1, and AD 360 means 360 years after the year AD 1. BC is written after the number of years and AD is written before.

The term BP (before present) is often used with scientific dating methods. But the present time is not static so scientists chose the year 1950 as the fixed point. This complicates matters as the term BP does not mean the actual present time. The years between 1950 and the present must therefore be added to any scientific date.

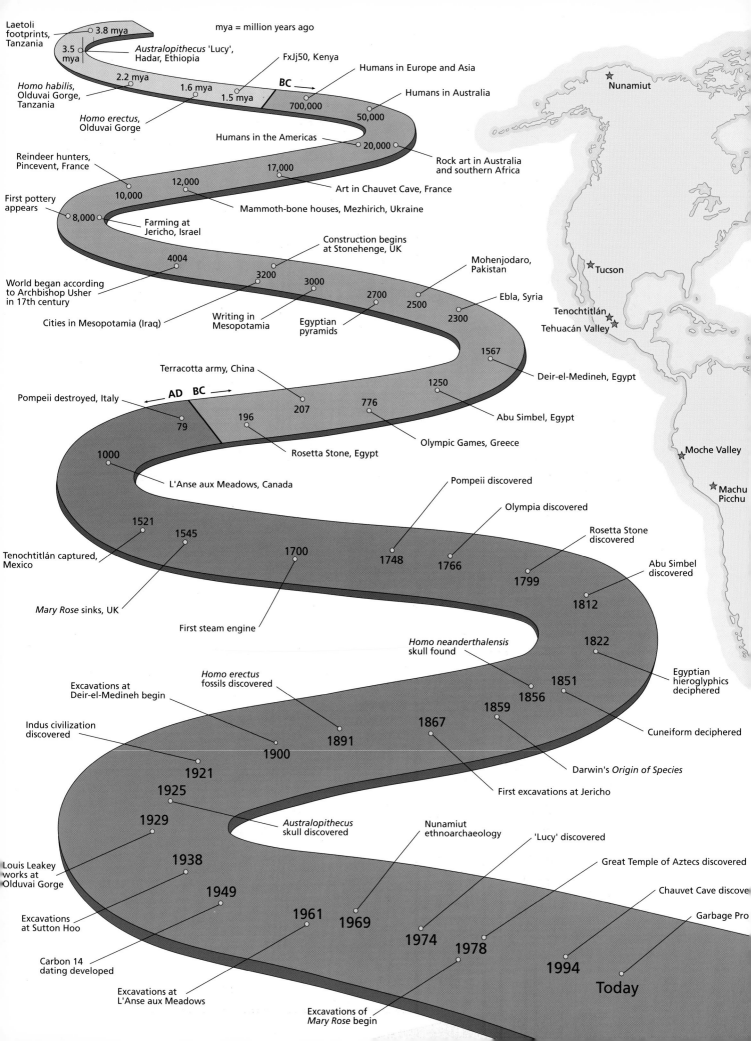

Laetoli footprints, Tanzania — 3.8 mya

3.5 mya

Australopithecus 'Lucy', Hadar, Ethiopia

mya = million years ago

FxJj50, Kenya

Humans in Europe and Asia

2.2 mya

Homo habilis, Olduvai Gorge, Tanzania

1.6 mya

1.5 mya

BC →

700,000

Humans in Australia

50,000

Homo erectus, Olduvai Gorge

Humans in the Americas

20,000

Rock art in Australia and southern Africa

Reindeer hunters, Pincevent, France

17,000

12,000

Art in Chauvet Cave, France

First pottery appears

10,000

Mammoth-bone houses, Mezhirich, Ukraine

8,000

Farming at Jericho, Israel

4004

World began according to Archbishop Usher in 17th century

Construction begins at Stonehenge, UK

3200

3000

Mohenjodaro, Pakistan

2700

2500

Ebla, Syria

Cities in Mesopotamia (Iraq)

Writing in Mesopotamia

Egyptian pyramids

2300

1567

Deir-el-Medineh, Egypt

Terracotta army, China

1250

Pompeii destroyed, Italy

AD BC →

207

776

Abu Simbel, Egypt

79

196

Olympic Games, Greece

Rosetta Stone, Egypt

1000

L'Anse aux Meadows, Canada

Pompeii discovered

Olympia discovered

Rosetta Stone discovered

1521

1545

1700

1748

1766

Abu Simbel discovered

Tenochtitlán captured, Mexico

1799

1812

Mary Rose sinks, UK

1822

First steam engine

Homo neanderthalensis skull found

Egyptian hieroglyphics deciphered

1851

1856

Excavations at Deir-el-Medineh begin

Homo erectus fossils discovered

1859

1867

Cuneiform deciphered

Indus civilization discovered

1891

Darwin's *Origin of Species*

1900

First excavations at Jericho

1921

1925

Australopithecus skull discovered

Nunamiut ethnoarchaeology

'Lucy' discovered

1929

Great Temple of Aztecs discovered

1938

Louis Leakey works at Olduvai Gorge

1949

Chauvet Cave discove

Excavations at Sutton Hoo

1961

1969

Garbage Pro

Carbon 14 dating developed

1974

1978

Excavations at L'Anse aux Meadows

1994

Excavations of *Mary Rose* begin

Today

Nunamiut

Tucson

Tenochtitlán

Tehuacán Valley

Moche Valley

Machu Picchu

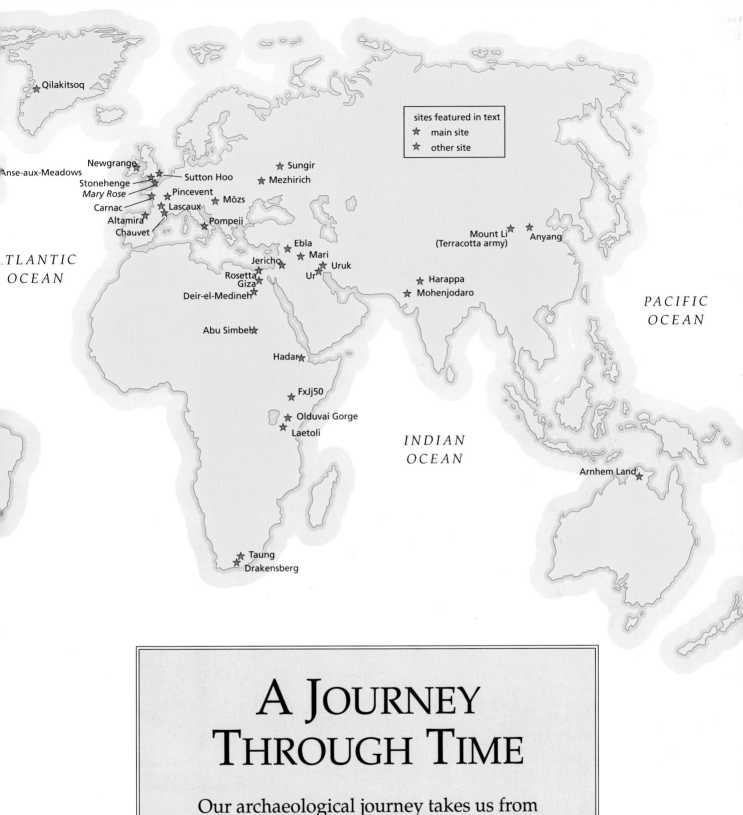

Qilakitsoq

Anse-aux-Meadows

Newgrange

Sutton Hoo

Stonehenge

Mary Rose

Carnac

Pincevent

Altamira

Lascaux

Chauvet

Pompeii

Sungir

Mezhirich

Mözs

Ebla

Mari

Jericho

Uruk

Rosetta

Ur

Giza

Deir-el-Medineh

Abu Simbel

Hadar

FxJj50

Olduvai Gorge

Laetoli

Mount Li
(Terracotta army)

Anyang

Harappa

Mohenjodaro

Taung

Drakensberg

Arnhem Land

ATLANTIC
OCEAN

PACIFIC
OCEAN

INDIAN
OCEAN

sites featured in text
★ main site
★ other site

A JOURNEY
THROUGH TIME

Our archaeological journey takes us from
3.8 million-year-old footsteps in Africa to
modern rubbish in America. We see how our
ancestors adapted to changing environments
and experimented with new ideas. The
monuments we see and the objects we find
are evidence of the inventiveness and creativity
of the human race.

IN THE BEGINNING

Nairobi

Our archaeological journey through time begins in Africa. More than 3 million years ago our earliest known ancestors roamed the landscape in parts of southern and eastern Africa. Evidence from these areas has shown how they and later humans developed and lived.

The first fossil hominid remains were recognized in South Africa in 1925 by Raymond Dart, an anatomist. He named them *Australopithecus*, the Latin word for southern ape, because they had many apelike features. They had small brains, but unlike apes they walked on two legs rather than four: they were bipedal. We therefore include them in our human family, although they are not fully human. In scientific language, humans form part of the hominid line of evolution and *Australopithecus* was the last of the prehuman hominids.

Homo habilis – handy man

Australopithecus, then, is our ancestor, but is too different from us to be considered really human. The first real humans appeared about 2 million years ago, once

△ The evolution of modern humans:
1 *Australopithecus* (southern ape) **2** *Homo habilis* (handy man) **3** *Homo erectus* (upright man) **4** *Homo neanderthalensis* (Neanderthal man) **5** *Homo sapiens sapiens* (modern humans).
As humans evolved, their way of life also changed and became more complex.

◁ Olduvai Gorge, Tanzania, with the extinct volcano Lemagrut in the background. Between 2 million and 800,000 years ago groups of our early ancestors moved about this area and set up camps along the shores of ancient lakes and rivers.

again in parts of southern and eastern Africa. Humans are given the Latin name of *Homo*, meaning 'man'. *Homo habilis*, or 'handy man', is the name given to the first real humans. Although not exactly like us, *Homo habilis* had many more human features than *Australopithecus*.

The first real human is called 'handy man' because we believe that this species broke and sharpened pieces of stone to use as tools. Very simple pieces of fractured stone have been found in the same places as bones of *Homo habilis*.

Some archaeologists maintain that *Australopithecus* also made stone tools, but we would need to find *Australopithecus* remains and stone tools together to have definite proof of this. No such finds have been made.

Adventurous *Homo erectus*

Remains of *Australopithecus* and *Homo habilis* have been found only in eastern and southern Africa. About 1.6 million years ago, another hominid appeared on the scene, *Homo erectus* or 'upright man'. This species looked more like us, although more strongly built. Apart from differences in physical appearance, there are other important differences between *Homo habilis* and *Homo erectus*. New types of stone tool have been found with *Homo erectus* remains; the most distinctive is a 'biface' or hand axe. This is a

pebble or large flake of stone which has been carefully prepared on each side to produce a regular shape and sharp edge.

We also believe that *Homo erectus* discovered how to make and use fire. Fire was important for a number of reasons: it meant that these early humans could keep warm in cold climates and it gave them greater protection from wild animals. Certain plants, such as roots and grains, are only edible if cooked. Control of fire allowed people to choose from a much wider range of plants to eat.

Homo erectus people did something that *Homo habilis* populations had never done: they travelled long distances. Remains of *Homo erectus* have been found not only in Africa but also in Asia, and as far afield as China and South-east Asia.

◁ Bifaces, also called hand axes, found at sites in Olduvai Gorge. They are large pieces of stone flaked on both sides, which archaeologists believe had many different uses. *Homo erectus* began to make and use bifaces more than 1.5 million years ago.

LUCY AND HER DIAMONDS

In November 1974, after a morning of looking for hominid fossils in the blistering heat of the Hadar region in northern Ethiopia, Don Johanson, an American palaeontologist, and his student, Tom Gray, were returning to camp for lunch. They walked slowly towards their jeep, scanning the ground for fossils. Suddenly Johanson noticed a familiar-looking bone: it was clearly hominid. Looking about them, he and Tom Gray saw hominid bones scattered all around. It was electrifying. They had made a momentous discovery.

Careful excavation at this site was to reveal the most complete *Australopithecus* skeleton ever found. The shape of the pelvis showed it was female. The shape of the leg bones and nature of the joints indicated she had walked upright. Her teeth showed she was about 20 years old when she died.

One of the most popular songs at the time was 'Lucy in the Sky with Diamonds' by a pop group called the Beatles. It was often sung at the campsite. Soon the skeleton became known as 'Lucy'. She is the most famous Lucy of all time.

More than 40 per cent of the skeleton had survived. As a result it has been possible to reconstruct most of the skeleton because bones on one side of the body are duplicated on the opposite side. Lucy was less than 1.1 m tall and may have weighed less than 30 kg. She had some human features: she walked upright and some features of her teeth were humanlike. But she also had many apelike features.

The remains of Lucy were the first of many *Australopithecus* finds which Johanson and his team made in the fossil-rich Hadar region.

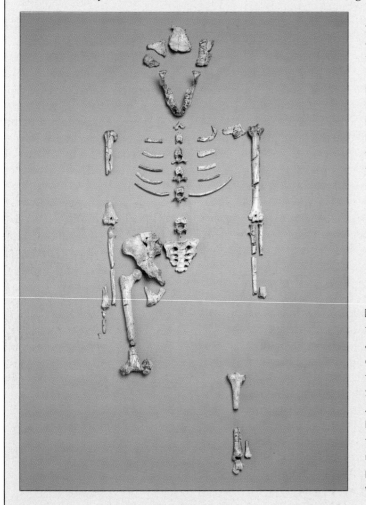

◁ *Australopithecus afarensis* (southern ape from Afar), nicknamed 'Lucy'. The face, jaw and brain size are apelike. Hip and limb bones indicate upright walking, but most experts believe these hominids continued to spend time in trees.

▷ Model of an adult female *Australopithecus africanus* (southern ape of Africa), reconstructed from remains found at Sterkfontein in South Africa. Like Lucy, this hominid was small (less than 1.3 m tall), weighed no more than 30 kg, and probably ate only vegetable foods.

◁ The formation of Olduvai Gorge: **1** About 2 million years ago early hominids roamed the area in search of food. **2** Sediments gradually filled the lake. During the last 500,000 years earth movements caused changes to the landscape and Olduvai Gorge was formed.
3 The layers of sediments and ash accumulated in the last 2 million years can be seen on the sides of the gorge today.

1

2

3

HOW THE FIRST HUMANS LIVED

By piecing together evidence from the bones of these various early ancestors, palaeontologists can reconstruct what they may have looked like. But how did they live? That is a more difficult question to answer, especially when we are dealing with life between 3 million and 1 million years ago. Indeed, it is a question that cannot be fully answered. However, archaeologists working in East Africa have filled many gaps in our knowledge about early humans.

Olduvai Gorge

Olduvai Gorge in Tanzania (see map on page 36) is rich in archaeological sites that cover the last 2 million years. Its secrets have been meticulously prised out by Louis and Mary Leakey, who spent over 50 years working at Olduvai, and by their son Richard, who has also worked on many other sites in Kenya. The work of this family and their teams of specialists has provided us with an immense amount of information about our early ancestors.

Today, Olduvai Gorge is like a huge gash in the flat Serengeti plains of northern Tanzania. Geologists and geomorphologists, who study the formation of land surfaces, have been able to draw a detailed picture of how Olduvai Gorge was formed. About 2 million years ago the landscape was quite different from that of today; streams from nearby volcanic highlands emptied into a large lake. Gradually the lake filled up with sediments deposited by the rivers and with ash that spewed out of erupting volcanoes. During the last 500,000 years, geological faulting – movements of the earth – caused a depression to form in the east of the region. A new river system, flowing towards the depression, began to cut through the deposits, so forming the gorge. The layers, or strata, of sediment and ash which filled the old lake are visible on the sides of the gorge. The many strata of volcanic ash can often be dated by various scientific methods.

Weather conditions over hundreds of thousands of years have caused parts of the walls of the gorge to wear away or erode. This continual process of erosion sometimes reveals stone artefacts and fossil bones, some of which may be the remains of meals eaten by early humans. Remains of *Australopithecus*, *Homo habilis* and *Homo erectus* have been uncovered at Olduvai. These three lines of evidence – fossil animal bones, stone artefacts and fossil hominid bones – demonstrate that our early ancestors roamed near the shores of the lake and by the many streams in the Olduvai region between 2 million and 1 million years ago.

△ Erosion often reveals stone artefacts and bones. At Hadar in Ethiopia the exposed bones of a fossil elephant are carefully excavated.

FOOTPRINTS FROM THE PAST

Laetoli is an area south of Olduvai Gorge in Tanzania, close to an ancient volcano. Almost 4 million years ago a series of small volcanic eruptions covered the area with hot ash. Shortly afterwards it rained. Migrating animals crossing the area left their footprints in the wet ash: hares, guinea fowl, elephants, pigs, rhinoceros, buffaloes, hyenas and antelopes. Three *Australopithecus* hominids also left their footprints: two adults, the second walking in the footprints of the first, and a child. The hot sun dried the ash and its precious prints. Later more ash fell, safely covering the footprints and preserving them for nearly 4 million years.

In 1976 they were discovered by Mary Leakey's team who were working in the Laetoli area. The shape of the footprints shows that they were made by upright walking hominids who walked much like modern humans. These are the oldest hominid footprints in the world. They have been studied with great care and casts of them have been made, but the originals have once again disappeared from sight. This time they have been covered deliberately in order to protect them from the destructive forces of erosion.

Looking for early sites at Olduvai

What happened when fossil bones or stone artefacts were found in the eroding walls of Olduvai Gorge? Mary Leakey usually dug one or more trial trenches to judge how far the archaeological material extended. Some sites had just a few artefacts, but others were rich in bones and stone artefacts and justified a larger excavation.

The Leakeys did not rely on erosion alone to reveal archaeological sites: they went out in search of them. They walked over the area scanning the ground for evidence of ancient human activity. It was through hours of such meticulous surface survey that most of the early sites in East Africa were discovered.

◁ Mary Leakey excavating at the site of Laetoli, Tanzania, in 1978 where the oldest hominid footprints in the world were discovered. Mary and her husband Louis excavated numerous sites in East Africa and unearthed the remains of many early hominids. In 1959 Mary found the skull of another species of *Australopithecus* who was nicknamed 'Nutcracker Man' by the press because of its massive teeth.

▷ Excavation of a cliff site at Olduvai Gorge where a hippo skeleton was found. The site, which dates to about 800,000 years ago, was located high on the side of the gorge and was revealed as erosion cut through the walls. The discovery of stone tools near the hippo skeleton suggests that humans (*Homo erectus*) obtained meat from it, although they probably did not kill the animal. Archaeologists carefully chip away the rock-hard sediments covering the bones.

Different types of site

The Leakeys excavated many sites at Olduvai Gorge. All belong to a period called the Lower Palaeolithic or Early Stone Age. It was a time when metals had not been discovered and people used stone to make tools. The pattern of bones and stone artefacts found at Olduvai sites led Mary Leakey to propose that different kinds of activities took place at different sites.

On some sites many bones and artefacts were quite densely packed in a small area. Sometimes hominid remains were also found. These she called 'living sites'; she felt they were places where early hominids stayed for more than a few days. At other sites parts of an elephant carcass were found together with some stone tools; these she called 'butchery sites'. Early hominids may perhaps have encountered a dead elephant and used their stone tools to get some meat. Stone artefacts and bones are often found mixed together along river beds, probably carried and deposited there by the action of fast-running rivers. At these 'river sites'

the patterning of bones and stones is not the result of ancient human behaviour.

As archaeologists began to identify different types of site, they began to paint a picture of how our early ancestors lived: dwelling together in certain places, hunting animals or scavenging meat from dead animals, bringing it home to share with other members of their group. All this seems normal and human, according to the way we think today. But was it really like that? Were the archaeologists right in their interpretation of the evidence? Were the bones and stone artefacts really carried to the sites by early hominids or did they arrive there in other ways?

How archaeological sites are formed

In the mid-1970s a South African archaeologist, Glynn Isaac, decided to study how archaeological sites are formed. He thought that many factors could cause stone artefacts and bones to end up in the same place. Bones could have been brought to the site either by early hominids or by carnivores,

especially hyenas. They could have been carried there by one agent (hominids or carnivores) but later scavenged by the other. Bones could have been broken by humans or animals. Rivers can carry bones and stones long distances, especially when they are in flood. This means that bones and stone artefacts found near ancient river channels may not have been deposited there by humans. Stones could have been broken by humans, but they can also break naturally when they bang against other stones, especially in rivers.

Isaac believed that sometimes early hominids took meat back to their home bases (Mary Leakey's 'living sites'), where they shared it with their group. But he felt that all the possibilities had to be studied in order to find out what caused bones and stone artefacts to end up at a particular place. With this in mind, he conducted excavations in the Koobi Fora area of Lake Turkana in northern Kenya. This is another region rich in Early Stone Age sites. All archaeological sites were given numbers to make recording easier. FxJj50 was one of the many studied by Isaac.

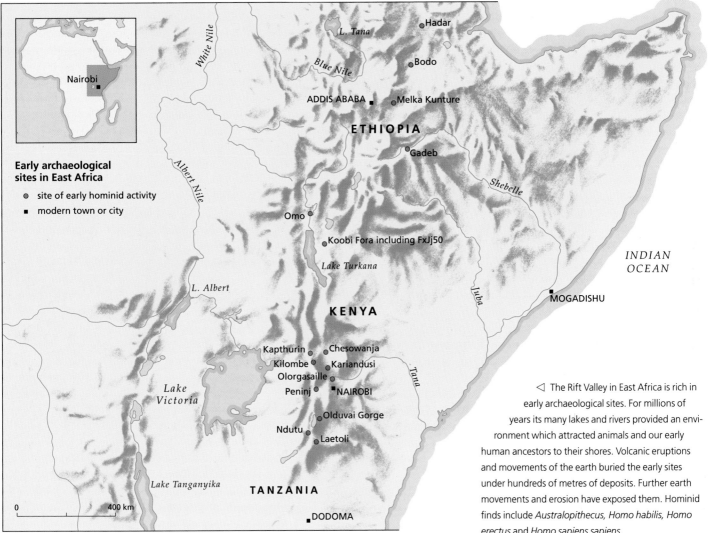

Early archaeological sites in East Africa

● site of early hominid activity

■ modern town or city

White Nile

L. Tana

Hadar

Blue Nile

Bodo

ADDIS ABABA ■ ● Melka Kunture

ETHIOPIA

● Gadeb

Albert Nile

Shebelle

Omo ●

● Koobi Fora including FxJj50

Lake Turkana

L. Albert

KENYA

INDIAN OCEAN

■ MOGADISHU

Juba

Kapthurin ● ● Chesowanja

Kilombe ● ● Kariandusi

Olorgasaille ●

Peninj ● ■ NAIROBI

Lake Victoria

Tana

● Olduvai Gorge

Ndutu ●

● Laetoli

Lake Tanganyika

TANZANIA

0 ——— 400 km

■ DODOMA

◁ The Rift Valley in East Africa is rich in early archaeological sites. For millions of years its many lakes and rivers provided an environment which attracted animals and our early human ancestors to their shores. Volcanic eruptions and movements of the earth buried the early sites under hundreds of metres of deposits. Further earth movements and erosion have exposed them. Hominid finds include *Australopithecus*, *Homo habilis*, *Homo erectus* and *Homo sapiens sapiens*.

The site of FxJj50

FxJj50 is a small site where about 1500 stone artefacts and 2000 bone fragments were found within a concentrated area. Because the site was small, Isaac felt that it might be the result of only one human occupation event. Early sites with many more bones and stone artefacts may well represent a number of human visits, and in such cases it is more difficult to separate different activities.

The stone artefacts and bone fragments at FxJj50 were found in a layer of volcanic ash. Scientists used a process called potassium argon dating to discover when the ash was deposited. They found that the ash was about 1.5 million years old. This date has been verified by other dating methods.

Geologists and palaeogeographers (those who study the geography of ancient landscapes) showed that early hominids

had set up their camp beside the bend of a stream and made stone tools from the stream cobbles. After the site had been abandoned, river floods covered the bones and stone tools with sediments and so preserved them.

Pollen studies revealed the type of vegetation in the area. The stream ran through grassland with some scrub, bushes and a few trees. More trees and bushes grew by the riverside, providing shelter from the elements and perhaps protection from wild animals.

Evidence from bones

Excavation began with test trenches to determine the extent of the site. A concentration of bones, stone tools, flakes and fragments was found in one zone. Different animals were represented among the broken bones: antelope, pig,

buffalo, horse, giraffe, hippopotamus. There were also the remains of crocodile, tortoise, baboon, porcupine, snake and catfish. Sometimes many parts of one animal were found; at other times just one part, for example a tooth, might have been the only evidence of a particular animal. Many bones were so fragmented that it was impossible to identify the animal to which they belonged.

Some bones which lay near each other could be 'refitted' (fitted back together). Such evidence suggested that whole animal carcasses had been brought to the site and broken up there. But who carried them in to the site and broke them up? One of the archaeologists looked at the bones through a microscope and saw that there were straight grooves on some, particularly on limb and rib bones. Under the microscope, marks made by animal teeth differ from those made by a sharp stone;

this means that human butchery of carcasses can be distinguished from the gnawing of bone by animals such as hyenas. Experiments in cutting meat from bones with stone tools demonstrated that the straight grooves were cut marks made by a sharp stone.

Other bones had been broken by hitting them with a heavy cobble, called a hammerstone, which causes them to break in a recognizable pattern. Why would anyone want to break into a bone? The answer is: to be able to get at the highly nutritious marrow in the middle. Animals sometimes break bones too, but these do not fracture in the same way as those broken by hammerstones. At FxJj50 the bone evidence (cut marks, breakage patterns and the pattern of bones on the ground) suggested that dead animals, or parts of them, had been brought to the site and eaten by hominids.

Evidence from stones

Archaeologists also looked at the broken stone. Like the bone pieces, many stone pieces could be 'refitted', which showed that they had been fractured at the site. Stones which have been 'knapped' (deliberately broken by humans) have special features that are absent from naturally broken stones. We can therefore recognize stones knapped by humans (artefacts). Many such stone artefacts were identified at FxJj50.

Isaac and his team believed that evidence from the bones and stones at FxJj50 shows that around 1.5 million years ago, early humans took meat to a shaded area by a stream, cut it up, and ate it there. It is difficult to say if they killed the animals themselves or if they scavenged dead carcasses, although scavenging seems more likely.

△ Excavation in progress at the site of FxJj50. Meticulous excavation and advanced scientific techniques have shown that 1.5 million years ago a group of hominids camped by a stream and made stone tools which they used to cut animal bones.

While it cannot be proved with certainty, Isaac believed that our early ancestors shared the food they found with other members of their group. This would be one of the earliest signs of the social behaviour that has characterized humans ever since the beginnings of developing humanity.

At this special site, therefore, we glimpse a moment in the distant past. Sites such as FxJj50 are not common. Isaac and his team have shown what the study of site formation processes (how a site is formed) can tell us, and how vitally important the information is to the interpretation of a site.

LIVING IN THE ICE AGE

The last great Ice Age – from about 100,000 to 10,000 years ago – occurred during a period known as the Palaeolithic. For most of this time large areas of the northern hemisphere were covered with enormous glaciers. People survived by hunting the many animals that lived in the vast plains and forests nearby.

The ice did not extend as far as central or southern Europe but winters there were still colder than they are today. Few trees grew near the ice but there were huge expanses of grassland called steppes, where woolly mammoth, woolly rhinoceros and wild ox roamed. Reindeer, horse, bison and wild goat grazed in the forests of river valleys that were more sheltered.

THE REINDEER HUNTERS OF WESTERN EUROPE

Pincevent is the name of an archaeological site on the banks of the Seine River in France. From 12,000 to 10,000 years ago the site was intermittently occupied by nomadic groups of men, women and children who set up camp there for a few weeks at the end of the summer. Why did they go there? What did they do? How did they survive? French archaeologists excavated the site to find answers to these questions, answers which lie among the bones and stones (ecofacts and artefacts) and other clues left on the ground by the nomads when they moved on. After the excavation the archaeologists were able to piece together a detailed picture of the activities of those ancient visitors.

The archaeology of Pincevent

Pincevent is what archaeologists call an 'in situ' site. This means that the stone and bone remains found during the excavations were in almost exactly the same position as when they were discarded thousands of years ago. By studying the stratigraphy of the site (the layers of deposits left by groups of people who occupied the site at different times), archaeologists have been able to reconstruct what happened in the area after each visit by the nomads.

The site is on very low-lying land next to the river. Each year, shortly after the camp was abandoned, the first snows probably fell, covering and protecting the remains of the camp during the harsh winter. In the following spring, water from melting snow and ice caused the river to rise and overflow its banks, gently flooding the site. As the water level sank it left a fine deposit of silts and muds which sealed in the archaeological material. This happened every year so that each visit to the site by the nomads was covered and separated from other visits. This sequence of events, in which each occupation by the nomads was followed by flooding, can be seen in the stratigraphy of the site.

△ Pictures of reindeer painted on cave walls by Palaeolithic artists. Reindeer herds would have been a common sight in Ice Age Europe.

◁ An artist's reconstruction of activities at Pincevent based on the archaeological evidence. The main activities centred around hunting reindeer and processing the catch as well as gathering plant food and cooking meals.

▷ An excavated area with reindeer bones (the remains of meals) and stone artefacts. Objects are not removed until their position and orientation have been carefully recorded and plotted on a map and photographs have been taken.

ARCHAEOLOGICAL METHODS USED AT PINCEVENT

On Palaeolithic sites excavators use a dental probe or something similar, and a fine brush to remove the soil, almost particle by particle, so that none of the evidence will be disturbed. At Pincevent all objects which appeared on the same level were at first left untouched and in place. When it was impossible to excavate further without disturbing those exposed on the surface, the archaeologists stopped excavating. The site was divided into squares, which were numbered; the position of each object was then recorded and plotted on a map. Photographs were taken of each excavated square with all the objects in place. In addition moulds were made of some of the squares which had important concentrations of objects. When all of this had been done the objects were carefully collected, wrapped and put in boxes to be taken to the site laboratory for further study.

In the laboratory many different types of maps were made from the excavation records. One map showed the position of all the objects, another only the stone tools, another the bones, another the hearths and so on. Archaeologists use these maps to help them to interpret the site, to discover what the artefacts mean in order to understand what happened in the past.

The specialists

Many specialists worked at Pincevent. Lithic analysts, studying the stone tools, looked for tools of particular shapes which would have been used for different purposes. They refitted pieces of flint together, rather like a jigsaw puzzle, and were often able to rebuild the complete pebble or block of stone (the 'core') from which the flint pieces had been struck.

Some archaeologists specialize in experimental flint knapping. They copied the work of the Palaeolithic flint knappers to understand what happens to a flint pebble during the manufacture of flint tools. Microwear analysts used very powerful microscopes to look for traces on the edges of flint which show what the tools were used for and how they were used. Archaeozoologists studied the animal bones and archaeobotanists studied the plant remains.

▽ Excavators work from raised wooden planks to avoid damaging any of the objects on the archaeological surface. They excavate with great care using fine tools.

▷ Antlers from a female reindeer and part of a reindeer jaw. Female antlers were rarely used for tools at Pincevent. Infomation from teeth and antlers has helped archaeologists determine when human groups were at the site. Specialists can discover the age of an animal from its teeth; those of three-month-old fawns were found at Pincevent. As it is known when reindeer give birth and when they shed their antlers, archaeologists have deduced that the hunters were at Pincevent in August and September.

Understanding the evidence

Nearly all the remains from Pincevent are either bone or stone. All parts of reindeer skeletons were found on the site. The abundance of reindeer bones suggests that the camp occupants were specialized reindeer hunters who brought the dead animals back to camp where they butchered them. It seems most likely that the families went to Pincevent at a particular time of the year specifically to hunt reindeer. The camp was well located. It was near an area where herds of migrating animals could easily cross the river on their way to winter feeding grounds.

Sharing the food

The camp occupants prepared and ate their food by the fireplaces or hearths on which they cooked the meat. Remains of burnt and unburnt reindeer bones were found around many hearths. It looks as though the reindeer meat was shared among all members of the hunting group and their families. Archaeologists have been able to fit together bones which were found at different hearths but which belong to the same reindeer.

Although reindeer meat was an important part of the daily diet, other food was readily available in the area. Excavations have uncovered evidence that hare, birds' eggs and fish were eaten, as well as wild plants, berries and roots.

Reindeer skins, teeth and antlers

What did these people do with the reindeer skins? No skins have survived but microwear studies on some flint artefacts indicate that they were used on reindeer hide. The families probably made clothes, blankets and coverings for their tents from the skins.

Reindeer teeth and antlers found at the site provide evidence about the time of year the hunting groups stayed there. Teeth can be used to determine the approximate age of an animal when it died. Some teeth found at Pincevent belong to three-month-old fawns. As reindeer give birth in May, these teeth indicate that the site was occupied in August. Reindeer antlers grow and shed (fall off) at special times of the year. The shed antlers at Pincevent show that the hunters were still there when it began to get cold, around late September.

Hearths

Fires from hearths leave tell-tale traces of charcoal which darken the ground. Several large and small hearths were excavated at Pincevent. Big stones, placed around the larger hearths, protected the fire. An extra large stone, often found on one side of a hearth, may have been a seat. Pieces of flint littered the ground around many hearths. These show that people made, repaired and used flint tools by the fires. We know from the bone remains that food was prepared, cooked and eaten at the hearths.

Charcoal from the hearths was used to date the site by the carbon 14 method (see pages 26–27). This evidence and that from teeth and antlers indicate that the site was occupied from about August to late September at different times between 12,000 and 10,000 years ago.

Flint artefacts

Through the study of flint artefacts, lithic analysts have been able to discover much about how the hunters made and used their stone tools. Most of the flint used by the Pincevent hunters is the same type of flint as the pebbles found in the river by the camp. However, some long, narrow pieces of flint called blades are made from a beige-coloured flint which is not found near the camp. This is much better flint than the local river pebbles. No waste pieces of the good, beige flint were found at the site. The hunters must have collected it at another camp, knapped (chipped) it there and brought the blades with them to Pincevent.

Microwear studies show that flint tools played an important part in everyday life at Pincevent. They were used to cut meat, to make antler tools, and to bore holes in wood, bone and shell as well as in small pebbles. They were also used to clean and prepare reindeer hides.

Other finds

Although most of the finds at Pincevent were reindeer bones and stone artefacts, a few other objects were found. Among these were a number of shells with a hole pierced through them, which were

REFITTING FLINT PUZZLES

By carefully refitting flint blades to the pebble (the core) from which they were struck, specialists have been able to piece together the original pebbles. They have learnt how the hunters made their tools, the problems they had and the mistakes they made. Some pebbles have been completely reconstructed except for one flake. This would have been the first flake removed by the knapper at the riverside when he tested the pebble to see if the flint was good.

Very often flint blades found in different parts of the site fitted together. We know then that people carried the blades to these places. Sometimes a pile of waste pieces was found a little away from the core and flint blades on to which they were refitted. In order to keep the area around the hearth clean and tidy, the knapper must have gathered up the waste, probably into some sort of container, and thrown it away. The refitting of stone artefacts from different parts of the site but which come from one occupation layer also provides evidence that the archaeological material belongs to one period in time, to one visit of hunters and their families.

Good and bad flint knappers

Modern-day experimental knappers have demonstrated that it is extremely difficult to make flint blades. Specialists studying the stone artefacts have identified tools which were made by good and bad knappers.

Archaeologists can learn a lot by studying the artefacts from one occupation layer – that is, the deposits left after one visit to the site by a nomadic

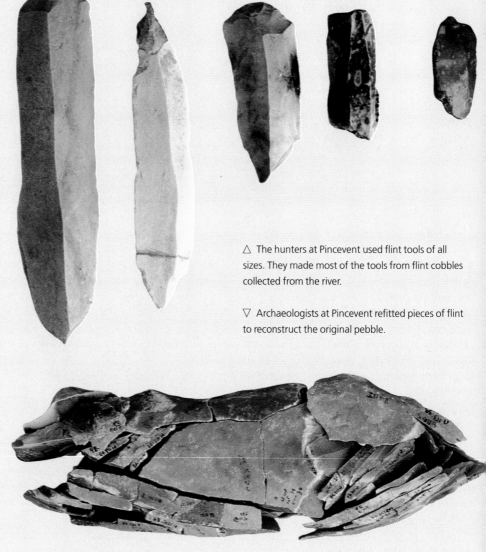

△ The hunters at Pincevent used flint tools of all sizes. They made most of the tools from flint cobbles collected from the river.

▽ Archaeologists at Pincevent refitted pieces of flint to reconstruct the original pebble.

group. Study of flint tools from one layer showed that a specialist flint knapper worked in the camp that year. No tool was too difficult for him to make. He knew exactly what he wanted and never made mistakes. He produced more flint blades from one pebble than anyone else in the camp. These razor-sharp blades were sometimes made into special tools or stored to be used later.

perhaps used as ornaments or good luck charms. A more intriguing find was the ochre (a red powder) covering much of the surface of the site. Did the hunters paint their bodies with it when they went hunting? We do not know.

The whole story?

Archaeologists from Pincevent have spent many years looking at the vast amount of evidence recovered from years of careful excavation. The story they have unravelled gives us a glimpse of life for a small community of hunters and their families thousands of years ago. It has been pieced together using methods such as those described here. We cannot hope to know everything that happened. For example, we do not know exactly what kind of clothes the people wore, what language they spoke or what they looked like. Nor do we know what kind of shelters they had, if any.

Pincevent is an unusual site to study as most artefacts and ecofacts did not move after the people left their riverside camp so long ago. We rarely get such a complete picture of a group working and living together in the Palaeolithic. Very often most of the evidence has disappeared. In such cases it is much harder to reconstruct past activities.

There were a few other good flint knappers in the camp, but none of them were as good as the master knapper and they did sometimes make mistakes. They usually made the tools needed for everyday use. Sometimes they made spear points from reindeer antlers and tied them on to wooden spear shafts. Using a special flint tool called a burin, they also made grooves along a piece of antler and stuck small flint blades into it.

Learning to make stone tools

Most people assume it must be easy to make stone tools such as those found on Palaeolithic sites. It is only when attempting to do so that they realize how difficult it really is. Experienced modern-day flint knappers have spent many years learning from others and practising on their own in order to improve their skills. It would have been no different in the past: children would have watched adult knappers and learnt from them.

The archaeologists who studied the collection of flint artefacts from Pincevent believe that some were made by older children learning to knap; it looks as though the better knappers showed them what to do. If true, this is the earliest evidence we have of a learning situation.

The refitting of flint blades has demonstrated that these teenagers often picked up a core from one hearth and took it away to a smaller hearth where they began to knap. Even the young children bashed flint pebbles together, trying to imitate their fathers. Needless to say they frequently made a mess of the pebbles.

△ Archaeologists have used evidence from the artefacts revealed in excavation to reconstruct three separate knapping activities which occurred around these two hearths. A good flint knapper walks away from the place where he had been making flint blades and working with antler. The waste flint forms a semi-circle in front of where he had sat. The knapper takes his blades with him but leaves the flint core and the antler which are no longer useful. The child, who had been watching him, picks up the core, walks to one side, sits down and practises knapping. The man who is seated had begun to work by the hearth at the bottom of the picture. He had thrown his flint waste to one side to keep his work area clean. Later he takes his core and walks to the top hearth where he continues knapping.

MAMMOTHS AND HUMANS IN EASTERN EUROPE

The landscape of eastern Europe, especially that region which is now the Ukraine, was extremely harsh and rugged during the last great glaciation. It was covered by vast, flat expanses of steppe. Beneath the steppe the ground was permanently frozen. This frozen layer of earth is called permafrost. In the bitterly cold winters, when temperatures were between 35°C and 40°C below freezing point, the steppe also froze and nothing grew. But in the short summers the temperatures rose, the surface snow and ice melted and the cycle of plant growth began once again.

Living in the steppes

A variety of large herbivores thrived in these cold conditions. Among them were woolly mammoth, woolly rhinoceros, bison, musk ox and reindeer. These huge herds of grazing animals provided enough food and fuel for groups of people to live well, even in the coldest of times.

Archaeological evidence shows us that people chose to live near large rivers. They constructed their settlements on land a little above the level of the river, which gave them an unrestricted view of the animals on the plains.

As there were very few trees they used animal bones, especially mammoth bones, to build their houses and to burn in their fires as fuel. One group of about 50 people lived at

△ Some of the many sites on the eastern European plains where mammoth-bone structures have been discovered. Mammoth bones were used for building and fuel because wood was scarce in the area.

Mezhirich, on the Dneipr River in the Ukraine, during the long, cold winters of 14,000 years ago.

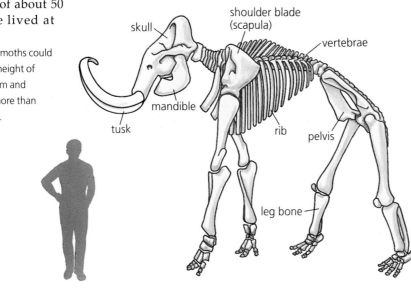

▷ Mammoths could reach a height of about 3 m and weigh more than 1000 kg.

skull
mandible
tusk
shoulder blade (scapula)
vertebrae
rib
pelvis
leg bone

The mammoth-bone houses of Mezhirich

The remains of five houses have been excavated. Mammoth skulls, placed side by side in a circle, formed the foundation of one house. Other bones were stacked on top of these, often in a special pattern. The spaces between the bones were filled with more bones and probably mud. Each house had two entrances: a main entrance and a back door. Two tusks, stuck into skulls, formed an arch at the front entrance of one house. Smoke escaped through a hole in the roof and probably through the back door, which would have been left open when the house was very smoky. Some of the mammoth bones were decorated in red ochre.

Archaeologists believe that the house frames were covered with mammoth hides, although these have not been preserved. We cannot be sure what the roofs were like. The archaeologist who first excavated Mezhirich believed they were dome-shaped.

Building a mammoth-bone house

Building mammoth-bone houses was indeed a mammoth task. It would have taken ten people almost six days to build one of the houses at Mezhirich. Mammoths were almost 3 m high and sometimes weighed more than 1000 kg. The partial remains of 149 mammoths were found at Mezhirich. The bones found in just one house weighed 21,000 kg all together. Some of the animals may have been hunted but the people probably also used bones from skeletons they found on the plains. They must have been very well organized to arrange the transport of the bones back to the camp.

Hearths and storage pits

Hearths were found inside the houses. Stone and bone tools as well as other pieces of bone were scattered around the hearths. A construction of bones, much like a bone barbecue, was found in one house. Evidence from bones shows that the people ate birds and fish as well as meat. It seems that, as at Pincevent, they swept the floors and threw the rubbish outside the house.

Hearths and work areas were discovered outside the houses as well as inside. There were also a number of pits that were dug deep enough into the ground to reach the underground permafrost layer. These would have been ideal places to store food – we could call them the first freezers in the world.

Tools, clothes and ornaments

Over 4600 flint artefacts were found at Mezhirich. Microwear studies show that some tools had been used to work on animal hides. Others had been used to make tools from mammoth ivory tusks and reindeer antlers.

Archaeologists think the people made and wore fur clothes. Bone needles and the skeletons of wolves and arctic foxes were found on the site.

Necklaces from seashells, amber and bone beads, and pendants from pierced wolf and arctic fox teeth, were also found. Seashells and amber come from far away from Mezhirich. How did they get there?

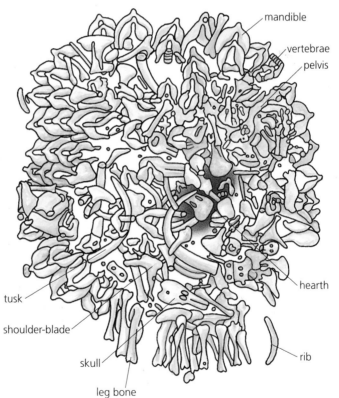

△ Reconstruction of a mammoth-bone house at Mezhirich. The outer wall consisted of 95 mandibles arranged in a pattern on top of a base wall of mammoth bones. A skull decorated in red ochre was near the entrance.

◁ The position of all the mammoth bones was plotted on a map during the excavation. The resulting plan formed the basis of the reconstructed house above.

We do not know. The Mezhirich people may have traded animal furs or mammoth ivory objects for these special goods.

The mammoth-bone houses themselves collapsed in time but they were quickly covered by a deep layer of loess. This is a fine dust from glaciers which is carried and deposited by the wind. Luckily for archaeologists, loess preserves artefacts well, and it is these artefacts that have told us so much about the people who lived at Mezhirich 14,000 years ago.

THE FIRST FARMERS

For their first 3 million years on earth our ancestors did not grow their own crops but moved from place to place in search of food. About 10,000 years ago they began to farm the land. It was a momentous development for humankind. People started to settle in one place; farming villages and small towns appeared. Ancient Jericho in the Jordan Valley was one such town.

The first humans scavenged meat from the bodies of dead animals, but later they began to hunt both large and small animals. They picked fruits and nuts from bushes and trees and dug edible roots out of the earth with wooden digging sticks.

However, a constant supply of food was not available in the same area all year round. People had to move from place to place in search of food. In winter, when it could be difficult to find much to eat, people must often have been hungry.

Domestication of plants and animals

About 10,000 years ago things very slowly began to change. People started growing their own crops and keeping their own animals – they began to farm. When archaeologists speak of domesticated plants they mean plants grown by farmers; when they speak of domesticated

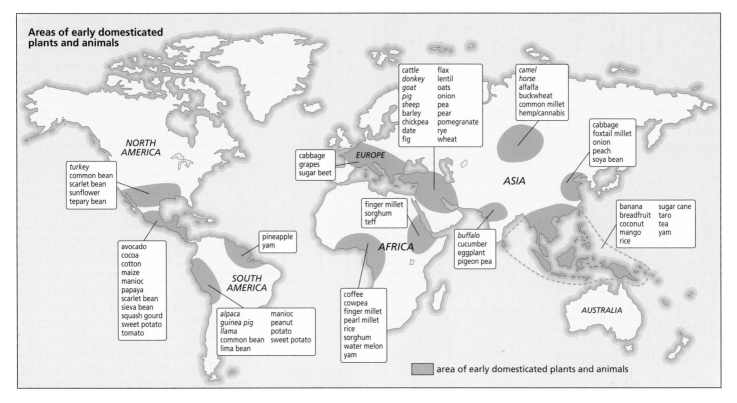

Areas of early domesticated plants and animals

NORTH AMERICA

turkey
common bean
scarlet bean
sunflower
tepary bean

avocado
cocoa
cotton
maize
manioc
papaya
scarlet bean
sieva bean
squash gourd
sweet potato
tomato

pineapple
yam

SOUTH AMERICA

alpaca   manioc
guinea pig   peanut
llama   potato
common bean   sweet potato
lima bean

EUROPE

cabbage
grapes
sugar beet

cattle   flax
donkey   lentil
goat   oats
pig   onion
sheep   pea
barley   pear
chickpea   pomegranate
date   rye
fig   wheat

AFRICA

finger millet
sorghum
teff

coffee
cowpea
finger millet
pearl millet
rice
sorghum
water melon
yam

camel
horse
alfalfa
buckwheat
common millet
hemp/cannabis

ASIA

cabbage
foxtail millet
onion
peach
soya bean

buffalo
cucumber
eggplant
pigeon pea

banana   sugar cane
breadfruit taro
coconut   tea
mango   yam
rice

AUSTRALIA

▭ area of early domesticated plants and animals

△ The domesticated plants and animals with which we are familiar today were first cultivated in many different parts of the world. Some, however, were developed independently in more than one area.

◁ Harvesting barley in Israel. In many parts of the world people continue to sow and harvest crops by hand. In ancient times sickles were made of bone or wood into which pieces of sharp flint were inserted. Today, metal scythes are used, but the method of harvesting is essentially the same.

animals they mean farm animals. In archaeology we call the period when farming began the Neolithic, or New Stone Age, because metal had not been invented. Tools were still made from stone as they had been in the earlier Palaeolithic or Old Stone Age. However, many Neolithic stone tools were made specially for farming activities.

Europeans have relied on wheat and barley as the main sources of plant food for thousands of years. Corn and beans have always been an important part of the daily diet in the Americas. In Asia rice and millet have long been the staple foods. Why did people begin to rely on different foods in different parts of the world? Quite simply because these were the plants which grew wild in their areas. It was the same with animals. Sheep and goats were domesticated in Europe, cattle in Asia and Africa, the llama and guinea pig in the Americas. Pigs were found wild over a much wider area, from Turkey to China, while dogs were found everywhere. Indeed, the dog has the distinction of being the first domesticated animal in the world.

How did farming affect people's way of life? It meant, above all, that they could store food to see them through the bad times of the year. They no longer needed

◁ Aerial view of the tell at Jericho in the Jordan Valley. The irregular surface is the result of the many excavations which have taken place there during the last 100 years. Excavations conducted by Dame Kathleen Kenyon in the 1950s revealed human occupation covering 10,000 years, including evidence about the first farmers who lived at Jericho.

▽ The tell at Jericho in the Jordan Valley rises above the surrounding plain. Tells are artificial hills which have formed over the centuries through the accumulation of layers of broken mudbrick buildings and their contents. The sequence of new buildings built on top of old ones on the same site is evidence of human occupation in the area over a very long period.

to roam around looking for food. In other words, they could settle in one place more or less permanently. Domestication of plants and animals first occurred in the Near East in a region known as the Fertile Crescent – a crescent-shaped area which extends from Israel to Turkey and Iran. Here the wild ancestors of European domesticated plants and animals were to be found. As we might expect, the earliest farming villages and towns arose in this area.

Tells, tepes and höyöks

As stone is rare in much of the Near East, people built their houses from sun-dried mudbricks. Mudbrick houses are not as durable as stone ones and often need to be repaired or even rebuilt. People built new houses on the ruins of older ones. Gradually, over thousands of years, artificial hills or mounds were formed consisting of layer upon layer of collapsed mudbrick houses and their contents. Such a hill is called a tell in the Middle East, a tepe in Iran and a höyök in Turkey. Many archaeological sites in the Fertile Crescent begin with one of these names. In this way we know that the site is part of an artificial hill.

Tells, tepes and höyöks are important because the many different layers form a stratigraphic sequence of evidence of past life. Stratigraphic sequences of layer upon layer of human occupation often cover a long period of time. In fact some tells have modern villages on top of them. In this case it is not always possible for archaeologists to excavate the tell as they would wish. Sometimes heavy rain or winds cause parts of the layers to move or collapse and become mixed up with other layers. Sometimes people in ancient times dug into lower layers looking for mudbricks to use for building. Or they made deep pits for their rubbish. Excavators can have a difficult job disentangling the mixed-up layers.

Excavating a tell

Tells can be very large. Full-scale excavation of an entire mound is impossible because it would be too expensive. Instead, the director of the excavation chooses parts of the tell to excavate. This is called sampling. A trench, rather like a

passageway, is cut into the tell. If the tell is very deep, the trench may be cut in steps to make the excavation safer. Some trenches may be small and not too deep, while others may descend to the bottom of the tell.

The massive tell at Jericho in the Jordan Valley has a long stratigraphy covering 10,000 years of human occupation. Although Jericho is well known as a biblical town, people had lived in the area for thousands of years before biblical times. The lowest levels of the tell have provided archaeologists with important information about the first groups of farmers who lived there.

THE FIRST FARMERS AT JERICHO

Ancient Jericho grew up around an oasis. Because of its perennial (year-round) springs the land was fertile and good for agriculture; it attracted many generations of farmers. People lived there from about 10,000 to 2000 years ago.

Today a large oval tell marks the site of ancient Jericho. It looks rather like a series of craters now because of the holes made by archaeological excavations. Over 100 years ago archaeologists began to excavate parts of the tell looking for the Jericho of biblical times. From 1952 to 1958 Dame Kathleen Kenyon, an English archaeologist, conducted a series of excavations and uncovered important evidence on the beginning of farming.

The Natufians

Farmers were not, however, the first people to be attracted to the lush area around the oasis. Deposits 4 m deep testify to the visits of hunting groups between 12,000 and 10,000 years ago. Archaeologists call these hunters Natufians. They were not farmers. Animal bones recovered from the Natufian layers of the tell are those of wild animals and the plant remains are of wild plants.

PPNA farmers come to Jericho

The people who came to Jericho after the Natufians occupied a much larger area around the oasis. They led quite a different

◁ Water gives life to dry areas. The land around Jericho, fed by the waters of the perennial springs, was fertile. Between 12,000 and 10,000 years ago hunters had exploited its resources, but they did not stay for long. From about 10,000 years ago groups of people began to settle there, attracted by the good soil and permanent water supply. They eventually began to cultivate crops and keep farm animals – they became farmers.

way of life. This period is known as the PPNA – the Pre-Pottery Neolithic phase A. It is called the Pre-Pottery Neolithic because the people at that time farmed but pottery had not yet been invented in the area.

For about 1000 years, generations of PPNA peoples lived at Jericho in round houses made of sun-dried mudbricks. The bricks of the PPNA houses are oval with a flat base and curved top. Kathleen Kenyon described them as 'hog-backed'. The houses have circular floor plans. The parts of the walls which still remain are slightly curved, indicating that the houses may have been dome-shaped. Sometimes a layer of cobbles was laid beneath the mud

floor. A mud step, covered with wooden planks, led down into the houses from outside. Although the wood rotted and disappeared long ago, its imprint is still visible in the mud. Many burnt wooden beams were found, showing that wood was often used in house-building.

The houses in one part of the site were partially destroyed. In place of the walls the excavators found layers of silt (tiny particles of clays and muds) and gravel (tiny river stones). A stream, which must have changed its course over time, passed through the houses. As the waters of the stream flowed onwards, the heavier silts and gravels fell to the bottom and formed the layers the archaeologists found.

THE ARTEFACTS FOUND AT JERICHO

Many different types of stone artefact were uncovered in the PPNA levels of the tell at Jericho. They include a variety of stone dishes, mortars, pestles and querns (hand-mills) for processing grain, and polished stone axes. It would have taken hours of grinding and polishing with grit and stone to make these artefacts.

The smaller flint tools include a few arrowheads and sickle blades. These are small flint blades which are placed in a wooden handle and used for harvesting plants. They often have a distinctive, shiny area along the edge; this is called sickle gloss, and is caused by the cutting of plants such as wheat and barley.

Obsidian, a glassy stone produced by volcanoes, was used for some tools. The obsidian came from Turkey, over 800 km away. Many tools made from animal bone were also found.

The PPNB people – farmers who occupied Jericho after the PPNA people had abandoned the site – made their dishes, bowls, querns, grinding stones and tools in stone, flint and obsidian, just as their PPNA predecessors had done. But they made them in different shapes. However, their bone tools are similar to those of the earlier levels.

◁ ▽ Plant processing tools found at Jericho. Stone pestles were used to grind grain in stone mortars.

Plants and animals in the PPNA levels

A few of the plant remains suggest that people were growing their own plants. Evidence of different types of wheat, barley, lentils, chick-peas, grapes and figs has been found. These are usually in charred form, which means that they were burnt or roasted by fire. Luckily for us roasting helps to preserve parts of the plant.

Some archaeologists do not believe that there were domesticated plants at Jericho in PPNA times. They say that there is very little evidence to prove it. Other archaeologists agree that not many domesticated plant remains have been found, but they still maintain that the stone mortars, pestles, querns and sickle blades show that people were processing grain. They also say that there would not have been enough wild food in the area to feed the population of PPNA Jericho. The people must therefore have grown some of their own food.

Most archaeologists agree that animals were probably not domesticated at this time. The animal bones from the PPNA layers are mostly those of gazelle but there are also bones of aurochs (wild cattle), wild goat, wild boar and fox. Hunting, then, must still have been the most common way of getting meat.

WILD OR DOMESTICATED?

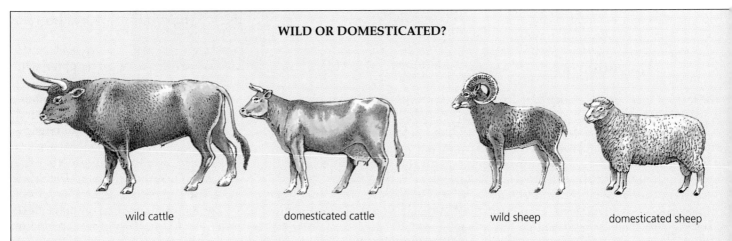

wild cattle   domesticated cattle   wild sheep   domesticated sheep

Domesticated and wild animals

Are there differences between wild and domesticated animals and plants that enable us to distinguish between them?

Domesticated animals often have smaller bones than their wild ancestors. In some animals tooth size decreased. Tusks and horns may be shorter and a different shape. Wool or hair coats are often shorter.

The wool of some domesticated animals, for example, sheep and llamas, can be spun and used to make woollen cloth.

The milk produced by domesticated cattle, sheep and goats can be drunk or turned into dairy products.

The stone wall and tower

The most outstanding feature found during the excavations was the remains of a huge stone wall, which must have surrounded the settlement. A stone ditch 2 m deep and 8 m wide runs outside the wall. Inside it stands an enormous stone tower, at least 8 m high and 9 m wide. A doorway leads to a staircase made of 22 stone slabs, each more than 1 m wide. The tower is covered by a roof of stone slabs. Small rooms close to the tower may have been used for storing grain.

Kathleen Kenyon felt that this wall and tower were built to defend the population from invaders. However, other archaeologists say that there is no archaeological evidence for warfare at this time and that the wall was erected to protect the town from floods and mud slides caused by heavy rains.

PPNA farmers leave Jericho

About 9300 years ago the PPNA settlement was abandoned. We are not sure what caused the people to leave. It is possible that the weather became much more arid, causing changes in the environment. The shortage of water, and its effects on the plants and animals in the region, could have made the people decide to move on.

▷ The tower at Jericho. A massive stone tower was built inside the stone wall encircling Jericho. At the bottom, a doorway leads to a stone-lined passage and staircase. Each huge stone step of the staircase had been specially prepared by hand with stone hammers. It is amazing to think that such a piece of architecture was built more than 8000 years ago.

Wild and domesticated plants

The grain or kernel of a plant is inside a protective case or husk called a glume. Glumes are attached to the stalk by a rachis. Each protected kernel and its rachis is called a spikelet.

The rachis in wild grains is brittle and breaks off very easily. When the grain is ripe the rachis will break off at the slightest wind and some grain may then be lost.

The rachis in domesticated plants is tough. The spikelets remain on the plants until they are harvested. This means that the grains can grow bigger than on wild plants.

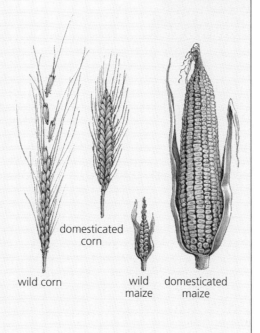

wild corn

domesticated corn

wild maize

domesticated maize

New groups of farmers at Jericho

The layers above the PPNA levels in the mound are those of the peoples who came to Jericho a few hundred years later. Like the PPNA populations, these new arrivals did not use pottery. However, as there are some differences between the two groups, archaeologists call the later settlements PPNB – the Pre-Pottery Neolithic phase B. The PPNB people stayed at Jericho for a long time. About 25 occupation layers have been found, which may represent a period of about 1000 years.

Some archaeologists maintain that the PPNB farmers emigrated to – or perhaps invaded – Jericho, bringing with them their own way of life. This would explain some of the differences (house shape, for example) between the PPNA and PPNB peoples. Other archaeologists reply that

△ A mudbrick made by the later farmers at Jericho. The brickmaker used his thumb to make a pattern on the flat, oval brick. These mudbricks are different from those of earlier occupation levels, which are rounded and have no pattern.

◁ In some houses round and square rush mats had been placed on the floors. The mats have disappeared but the mud floors bear their impression. These impressions are so clear that it is easy to distinguish the weave of the mats.

RITUAL AND BURIAL AT JERICHO

In both PPNA and PPNB times the people usually buried their dead deep beneath the house floors. In PPNA levels many human skulls were separated from the bodies and buried in specially arranged groups. Kathleen Kenyon thought this might indicate a cult of skulls, perhaps a type of ancestor worship.

The most spectacular finds in the PPNB levels have been the burials.

there are many similarities between the two groups (their farming implements, for example). These could mean that Jericho was reoccupied by people who were like the PPNA populations, but whose way of life had gradually changed over time.

Mudbrick houses of the PPNB

PPNB mudbrick houses are rectangular in shape. The mudbricks are flat and oval, with a pattern on top made by the thumbprint of the brickmaker. Many

small rooms without doors were probably used as storage rooms. The clay floors of the houses were plastered, often painted red or cream and sometimes covered with round or square rush mats. These mats have disappeared but impressions of them are imprinted on the mud floors. Similarly, impressions of reeds on chunks of the mud roofs which have collapsed on to the floors are evidence of their use in building. Drains ran outside the houses and troughs collected precious rainwater.

The plants and animals

Remains of domesticated plants and animals are more common in the PPNB levels. In addition to those found in the PPNA levels, a few new species make their appearance. Beans began to be grown as well as another variety of wheat; domestic sheep and goats appeared. However, people still collected wild plants and hunted wild animals. They could not yet meet all their needs through farming.

A number of human skulls were found that had been given special treatment. These were covered in plaster which was carefully moulded, perhaps into a portrait of the dead person. Shells were placed in the eye sockets, making them look very lifelike. Some skulls had painted hair and headdresses.

Other PPNB finds give us some clues about religious practices of the time. The unusual shape of a room found in one building suggests it may be a temple; a specially shaped stone found in a niche in a room in another building may be a shrine. A number of clay figurines, in human and animal shapes, and tiny greenstone lucky charms may also point to some kind of religious belief.

◁ A plastered skull from Jericho with cowrie shells as eyes. Many plastered skulls with carefully moulded features were found at Jericho. The special treatment given to these skulls suggests that they may have had some religious significance.

Local and long-distance trade

Many of the artefacts found in the PPNB layers of Jericho came from other areas in the Fertile Crescent and beyond. Obsidian came from Turkey, greenstone from northern Syria, shells from the Mediterranean and the Red Sea. There was no money, as we know it, at that time. How did the people pay for these goods? We cannot be sure, but we think they must have traded their own special goods, or perhaps food.

THE SEARCH FOR CORN IN MESOAMERICA

Mesoamerica is the term used by archaeologists for that part of Central America which includes southern Mexico, Guatemala and Honduras. Here the Olmec, the Maya and the mighty Aztec civilizations flourished long before the area was invaded and conquered by the Spanish in the early 16th century. Archaeologists have studied the beginnings and growth of farming in Mesoamerica to help them understand how these civilizations developed.

Corn, also called maize, is eaten throughout the region. Where was it first domesticated? Richard MacNeish, an American archaeologist, set out to answer that question. His research work showed that corn was farmed more than 5000 years ago in Mexico. But Mexico is a large country. Where was he to begin? MacNeish and his research team knew that the ancestor to wild corn grew in highland regions. Evidence of human occupation, including any plant remains, would most likely be preserved in dry caves. He therefore decided to focus his search on dry caves in highland regions.

▽ Ancient corn cobs. Corn was cultivated in Mexico about 7000 years ago. Early cobs were tiny.

A successful exploration

MacNeish began to explore the Tehuacán Valley in southern Mexico in 1960. He travelled by car and on foot around the valley looking for sites. If a place looked promising, he excavated a small area called a test pit to check for any signs of occupation. Success came at last in Coxcatlán cave with the discovery of three tiny corn cobs, each 2–3 cm long. These tiny cobs were the ancestors to our modern corn.

Between 1960 and 1963 MacNeish and his team found 454 sites. They collected 250,000 clay artefacts, 13,000 stone artefacts, 25,000 remains of domesticated plants, 80,000 remains of wild plants, 11,000 animal bones, 25,000 shells and 70 human burials.

The plant remains that were found included over 24,000 specimens of corn or maize. These specimens show how corn evolved and changed over time. The earliest cobs were less than 2.5 cm long. By the time of the Spanish conquest corn cobs were about 13–15 cm long.

Excavation in this way allowed MacNeish and his team to produce a picture of life in the Tehuacán Valley from around 10,000 BC to the Spanish conquest in AD 1521.

STONE GIANTS

Between 6500 and 3500 years ago farming communities in western Europe left highly visible signs of their presence in the form of huge monuments built with massive blocks of stone.

These monuments, known as megaliths (from the Greek *megas* 'large' and *lithos* 'stone'), are found in many places in the world but the oldest are in western Europe. Excavations often reveal burials inside, beneath or close to megalithic monuments. This has led archaeologists to interpret them as places of special significance for the burial rituals followed by farming societies in the area. A huge circular burial mound of stones and turf rises 11 m above the landscape at Newgrange in southern Ireland. A passage, lined and roofed with massive stones, stretches 24 m into the base of the mound, ending in three stone-lined chambers. On certain days the rays of the rising sun penetrate the passage and illuminate the central chamber at the back.

The immense size of the megalithic monuments, their imposing presence in the landscape and the labour needed to construct them suggest that some, at least, were also important as ceremonial centres for the early agricultural communities in Europe during the Neolithic and Early Bronze Age periods. At Carnac in Brittany rows of standing stones stretch several kilometres across the land. Today 3000 of the original 10,000 stones remain. Although no burials have been found under the Carnac stones, there are many megalithic tombs nearby.

Construction of these huge stone monuments continued for almost 3000 years, from the fifth to the second millennium BC. Since then, these stone giants which dot the landscape in so many areas have

▷ Interior of the passageway of the great megalithic monument at Newgrange in Ireland. The passageway is lined with huge stones (called orthostats), some engraved with patterns. It leads to a chamber designed in the form of a cross. Newgrange is dated to about 3100 BC.

◁ Carnac in Brittany, France, is an area with many megalithic monuments. At Le Menec there are 11 parallel lines of stones over 1 km long which date back to the middle of the third millennium BC. Archaeologists do not know why these stones were erected but think they must have been used for important ceremonies.

become shrouded in mystery and surrounded by legends and fantasies. They have attracted streams of visitors over the centuries.

The massive standing stones of Stonehenge, perhaps the most famous megalithic structure, dominate Salisbury Plain in southern England. It is one of more than 500 stone, wood and earthen monuments which lie within about an 8 km radius of Stonehenge itself.

STONEHENGE

From the ground Stonehenge looks like a jumble of upright and fallen stones, but from the air its design becomes clear. It is a series of circles within circles, some made of earth, others of large and small stones. A single stone (the Heel Stone) stands by the entrance as though guarding the monument. The faint lines of a pathway (the Avenue) lead into the distance.

Plan of Stonehenge today

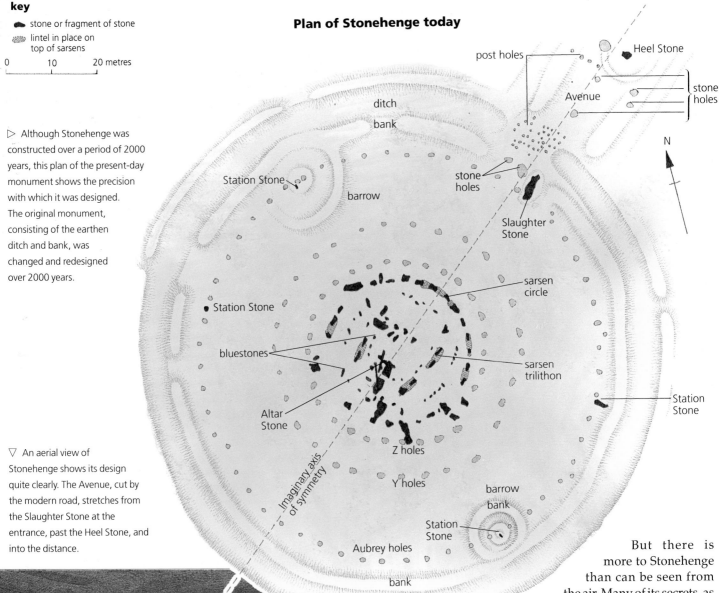

key

- stone or fragment of stone
- lintel in place on top of sarsens

0   10   20 metres

▷ Although Stonehenge was constructed over a period of 2000 years, this plan of the present-day monument shows the precision with which it was designed. The original monument, consisting of the earthen ditch and bank, was changed and redesigned over 2000 years.

Labels on plan: post holes · Heel Stone · Avenue · stone holes · N · ditch · bank · Station Stone · barrow · stone holes · Slaughter Stone · sarsen circle · Station Stone · bluestones · sarsen trilithon · Station Stone · Altar Stone · Z holes · Y holes · Imaginary axis of symmetry · barrow bank · Station Stone · Aubrey holes · bank · ditch

▽ An aerial view of Stonehenge shows its design quite clearly. The Avenue, cut by the modern road, stretches from the Slaughter Stone at the entrance, past the Heel Stone, and into the distance.

But there is more to Stonehenge than can be seen from the air. Many of its secrets, as well as those of the surrounding landscape, have been revealed through careful survey and archaeological excavations during the last 400 years. As a result archaeologists have been able to produce a detailed plan of the monument. Three circles of holes (Aubrey, Y and Z holes) separate the outer earthen bank and ditch from the inner circles of large and small stones. The central part of the monument is completed by two horseshoes of stones and a central stone, the Altar Stone.

Two further features called barrows can be seen at opposite sides of the enclosure inside the bank. (These are the sites of the two remaining Station Stones – see below.) Barrows are mounds of earth which often covered burials; they are common throughout the Stonehenge area. Over the years researchers have given names to the various features of Stonehenge and numbered the stones and holes to make the site easier to study.

The outer circles

The ditch and earthen bank form the largest circle at Stonehenge. Deer antler picks found during excavation of the ditch show that workers used these to dig the ditch deep into the chalky ground. They made the high bank with the earth and chalk they dug up, probably using skin or wicker baskets to move the rubble.

Just inside the ditch is the circle of 56 Aubrey holes, named after John Aubrey who discovered them in the 17th century. He was the first person to study the Stonehenge area in detail. He noted depressions in the ground, but it was not until the 1920s that some were finally excavated and discovered to be round pits. Many contained cremation burials. Flint artefacts and bone pins were found in the top layers of others. Excavation has shown that the Aubrey holes never held large stones or wooden posts. Similar holes have been found throughout the Stonehenge landscape; some archaeologists have interpreted them as pits for ritual offerings.

The 'Y' and 'Z' holes were also discovered during excavations in the 1920s. No one knows their purpose. It has been suggested that they were holes in which stones stood but no stone fragments have been found in any of them.

The large stone circle

The largest stones at Stonehenge are cut from a hard sandstone rock called sarsen. The sarsens are huge, weighing as much as 45,000 kg (the weight of nine male elephants) and measuring up to 7 m long.

Today the large, central circle consists of 17 gigantic standing sarsens, although fragments of stone and evidence of large holes indicate that originally there were 30. The tops were linked by a ring of horizontal sarsens called lintels. Specially prepared holes are visible at each end of the lintels, on the under side. These fit snugly into knobs on the tops of the standing sarsens. Although most of the lintels have now fallen, it seems that the

standing sarsens and the lintels were once firmly joined together to form a circle.

The standing sarsens are also slightly shaped, tapered towards the top, making them appear taller than they really are. The lintels are slightly curved to maintain the line of the circle. Great care was clearly invested in the cutting, shaping and smoothing of the stones at Stonehenge, which was done using only stone tools.

The bluestone circle

A smaller circle of bluestones stands inside the sarsen circle. The smaller stones, called bluestones because of their bluish colour, still weigh up to 4000 kg. Although few remain today, fragments of stone in the stone sockets and empty sockets indicate that there may originally have been up to 82 bluestones. Many have, however, fallen or been broken by the weight of sarsens falling on them. Some have been eroded by wind and rain, and others have been hauled away for other uses over the centuries. Sometimes excavation has revealed just the buried section of a stone. Signs of specially prepared holes and projections suggest that the bluestones may once have been joined together, but we cannot be sure if they formed a single circle or two circles, as some archaeologists believe.

△ We can easily imagine what the Stonehenge circle of sarsens and the trilithon horseshoe setting must have looked like. Little remains of the smaller bluestone circle.

▽ The projecting knob (tenon) on top of an upright sarsen was made to fit into a hole (mortice) on the under-side of a lintel. The precision of these mortice and tenon joints is astounding.

The horseshoes

The largest sarsens at Stonehenge form a horseshoe shape within the bluestone circle. This consists of five sets of trilithons – two standing stones joined by a lintel. (Trilithon means three stones in Greek.) The largest trilithon rises majestically in the middle of the horseshoe. The standing stones are shaped like those in the outer sarsen circle, and it seems that the lintels were attached to them in the same way. The shapes of prehistoric axes and daggers have been carved on some of the giant trilithons, but archaeologists are not sure what meaning these would have had for the prehistoric farming communities.

A smaller horseshoe of bluestones stands inside the large horseshoe. In the centre of these bluestones lies another sarsen, the Altar Stone, which originally stood upright. This stone lies on the axis of symmetry, an imaginary line which divides Stonehenge in half.

The Station Stones and Slaughter Stone

A few other stones, some still in place and some missing, complete the arrangement at Stonehenge. Four smaller sarsens (the Station Stones) were originally placed

inside the bank. Two remain – although one is only a broken stump – and small mounds cover the holes for the missing ones. The function of the Station Stones is unclear, but some researchers believe they were used as astronomical markers by the ancient farming communities.

A large fallen sarsen at the entrance to Stonehenge was ominously called the Slaughter Stone because of the red stains on its surface, thought to be the stains of sacrificial blood.

The truth is far less dramatic: the staining is due to particles of iron in the rock which turn red when the rock is wet. In addition, the stone had not originally been placed flat on the ground but had been upright. Two further holes were found nearby: these show that other stones stood at the entrance with the Slaughter Stone.

The Heel Stone and the Avenue

The Heel Stone stands outside the enclosure in the Avenue. Excavation in 1980 revealed another hole near the Heel Stone where a second stone may have stood. The imaginary axis of symmetry for the monument runs between these two stones. Recent excavations have revealed further stone holes between the Slaughter Stone and the Heel Stone along this imaginary line. A number of smaller holes found between the entrance and the Heel Stone may have held wooden posts.

A ditch and earthen bank line the sides of the Avenue, stretching away from the entrance of Stonehenge for 3 km. The Avenue, noted in 1721 by the archaeologist William Stukely, may have been a path along which processions moved to and from Stonehenge.

▽ Thousands of years of erosion by weathering have affected the stones at Stonehenge. But the projecting part of the lintel on the left, which would have slotted into the next lintel, is still visible.

▷ The Heel Stone guards the entrance to Stonehenge. This picture was taken in the middle of winter, but Stonehenge is impressive no matter what time of year we see it. How much more impressive it must have been to those who saw it about 3500 years ago when the monument was complete and all the stones in place. It is not difficult to imagine processions, perhaps led by a priest or priestess, slowly moving through the entrance to begin midwinter ceremonies.

HOW OLD IS STONEHENGE?

Archaeologists have got some absolute dates using the carbon 14 (C-14) method (see page 26). In addition artefacts which are characteristic of certain periods have provided relative dates (see page 24). In this way archaeologists have worked out a sequence of construction stages for Stonehenge. Although some stages can be dated with reasonable confidence, we cannot be absolutely certain in which order some of the building stages occurred. However, we are sure that Stonehenge was built over a long period, between around 3000 BC and around 1000 BC.

C-14 dates from an antler found at the bottom of the ditch indicate that the ditch and bank were the first part of Stonehenge to be built, around 3000 BC. C-14 dates for charcoal in one of the Aubrey holes suggest that these had been dug by at least 2200 BC, although some archaeologists claim an earlier date of around 2700 BC. We must remember that the C-14 method dates

the charcoal but not the actual pit itself: we can be sure only that the holes are older than the dated charcoal found in them. Bone pins and flint artefacts found in some holes are typical of those found in Late Neolithic sites, so providing us with a relative date for the holes themselves.

There was little activity at Stonehenge between 2550 BC and 2150 BC. Snail shells found in one stratum of the ditch are from woodland species, indicating that the area was wooded at that time.

C-14 dates show that construction of the Avenue began about 2150 BC. It has been suggested that the Heel Stones may also have been erected at this time.

The sarsens were set in place between about 2100 BC and 1800 BC. Although archaeologists are not sure in what order the stone circles were constructed, they believe the sarsens were erected after the Aubrey holes had been dug and before the final placing of the blue-stones. Some people believe the

bluestones were part of an earlier construction which was dismantled and reused in the final circle and horseshoe, dated to 1800 BC.

Despite the problems of dating, we know that the monument was completed by about 1500 BC when the Y and Z holes were dug. A C-14 date from the Avenue ditch shows that it was extended between 1200 and 1000 BC. Stonehenge, then, was used in prehistoric times for almost 2000 years.

◁ Reindeer antler picks such as this were used to dig the ditches at Stonehenge. Some also provided C-14 dates.

△ **1–3** Erecting a sarsen, using rollers, ropes and scaffolding. **4–6** Raising a lintel. It may have been placed on a log platform, raised by adding logs under it, and when high enough, slid on to the sarsens.

▷ An artist's reconstruction of what Stonehenge may have looked like when all the stone settings were in place (about 1500 BC). It is possible that the bluestones had been placed in different positions before the final setting.

How were the stones transported to Stonehenge?

Neither sarsens nor bluestones are found near Stonehenge. The closest source of sarsens is 30 km away. How could people have moved these huge stones over hilly country, especially at a time when the wheel was unknown. Archaeologists believe the sarsens may have been dragged to Stonehenge on sledges which moved over a series of wooden rollers. These sledges could have been pulled by people, by oxen or by both.

In 1923 a geologist discovered that most of the bluestones came from the Preseli mountains in Wales, more than 200 km away. Nobody knows how they were transported to Stonehenge. Some archaeologists have suggested a journey partly by boat and partly by land. Another suggestion is that the bluestones may have been transported by powerful sheets of ice during the Ice Age thousands of years before. If this theory is correct, then the builders of Stonehenge would not have had to pull the stones far. However, no bluestones have been found anywhere near Stonehenge and it seems unlikely that every available bluestone in the area was used for the monument.

How did the builders get the stones in place?

There were no mechanical cranes or huge lifting machines to help the Stonehenge people set the massive stones in place. They had to do it by hand.

In 1901 one of the large sarsens was tilting so dangerously that it had to be replaced in its original upright position. The restoration process revealed some details about how the stones had first been erected. The workmen dug a deep hole into the chalky ground with antler picks. They made one side straight but formed the other into a gently sloping ramp down which they slid the sarsen. When it was in the hole they pulled it upright, then filled the hole with stones, chalk and earth to stabilize the stone. We do not know how the sarsens were levered upright when Stonehenge was first built, but some people think the builders may have used a system of ropes and wooden scaffolding.

Some of the original tools were found among the rubble in 1901: flint tools, fragments of antler picks, large and small stones used as hammers, including huge sarsen hammers weighing 18–27 kg. With these the builders cut, shaped and smoothed the stones. No metal tools were used.

We do not know how the Stonehenge builders got the lintels on top of the standing stones. The diagram above (4–6) illustrates one theory. Whatever method was used it would have taken considerable time to raise the lintels.

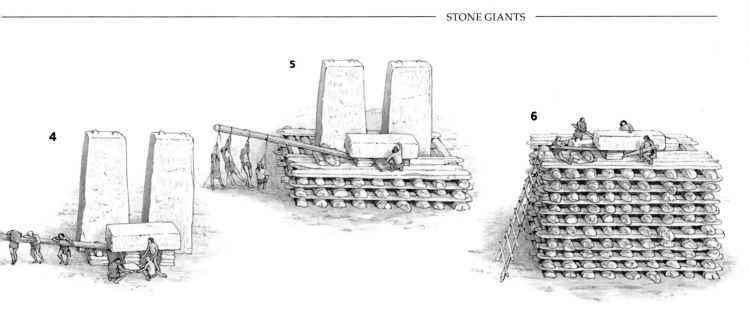

What happened at Stonehenge?

Stonehenge is one of hundreds of monuments on Salisbury Plain. Some have circular banks and ditches similar to Stonehenge, others consist of round or long barrows. Other strange monuments called *cursi* consist of parallel banks and ditches. The longest, built 500 years before Stonehenge, is more than 2.8 km long and 100 m wide. It was discovered in 1723 by William Stukely, who thought it was used for horse races in Roman times; he gave it the Latin name for a racecourse, *cursus*.

Most archaeologists agree that the monuments must have been used for ceremonies. Burials have been found in many sites, although few artefacts have been found with them. The larger enclosures such as Stonehenge may have been places where farming communities assembled on special occasions, especially at the midsummer and midwinter solstices. The midsummer sun rises and the midwinter sun sets along the axis of symmetry of the monument. Perhaps the Stonehenge people had ceremonies to celebrate the fertility of the land which, through their crops and animals, gave them life. We know for sure that, contrary to popular beliefs, Druids did not build Stonehenge for their religious ceremonies. It had been abandoned for many centuries before the Druids appeared in England.

The building of Stonehenge and other huge monuments was a massive undertaking that required millions of hours of work. Some archaeologists suggest that these monuments could have served as territorial markers. They would indicate the boundaries of an area controlled by a powerful chief.

We do not know what happened at Stonehenge but we can make plausible interpretations on the basis of the evidence we have already found. Future archaeological survey and excavation will undoubtedly add to the store of information about Stonehenge which has been accumulating over the last 400 years.

▽ Stonehenge, like many megalithic monuments, was designed so that the sun rose and set in a particular spot during the midwinter and midsummer solstices.

MOHENJODARO
AN ANCIENT CITY

Cities sprang up along the Indus River in Pakistan 4500 years ago. Mohenjodaro is one of the most important of these settlements. Excavations have revealed a wealth of information about the so-called Indus civilization, though much still remains a mystery to us.

Today, every country has large and small cities. We see them on the television and in films, we read about them in books, magazines and newspapers, we learn about them in school. We know that cities are not all the same: some are bigger than others, some are more important. They look different in many ways. Streets can be wide and straight or narrow and winding. Some cities have many parks, others very few. When we visit a foreign city it may feel different. But if we look at cities more closely we will find that they have a number of aspects in common. They are centres with a much larger population than elsewhere. They have many buildings, not only houses and apartments but also big buildings such as palaces, government buildings and large places of worship. There are also industrial areas where goods are manufactured, and shopping areas where goods can be bought.

◁ Modern-day view of the Indus River. For thousands of years people have fished in the Indus, irrigated their fields with its waters and travelled along it. Four thousand years ago it flowed near the ancient city of Mohenjodaro. Since then it has changed its course: today it is over 3 km away.

▷ The site of Mohenjodaro is so large (more than 2.5 sq km) that only parts of it have been excavated. The excavated areas and unexcavated mounds can be seen here.

The first cities

The first true cities evolved about 5000 years ago along the Euphrates and Tigris rivers of ancient Sumer, now part of modern Iraq. By 4500 years ago cities had begun to spring up in other areas as well, along the banks of the River Nile in Egypt and along the Indus River and its tributaries in Pakistan.

Early cities in all these areas shared the same features as those listed above for modern cities: densely populated living areas, large, impressive buildings, shops and manufacturing areas. Careful channelling of rivers changed the once dry land around these early cities into fertile fields which produced more than enough food for the local population. Huge walls often encircled the cities to protect against enemy attacks. Within the walls stood magnificent temples and palaces of the city priests and rulers, as well as blocks of smaller houses where most of the ordinary people lived.

At about the same time as these first cities developed, writing was invented. Some documents were written on clay which was baked by fire or dried in the sun. Others were carved in stone or written on paper called papyrus. Using the information from these written documents and that from careful excavation, archaeologists have been able to reveal the secrets of many ancient cities which today are often only ruins in the sand.

Discovery of ancient cities

The presence of ancient cities has been known for hundreds of years, although extensive excavation has occurred only in the last 100 years. The early cities of Sumer and the Indus were hidden under shifting sands and mud deposited by flooding rivers. The rivers themselves have changed their course so that today these lost cities may appear as mounds in a deserted landscape, some distance from the rivers. Sometimes, however, written records refer to particular places, giving the archaeologist clues on where a city might be found. But quite often discovery of these ancient cities is more a question of luck.

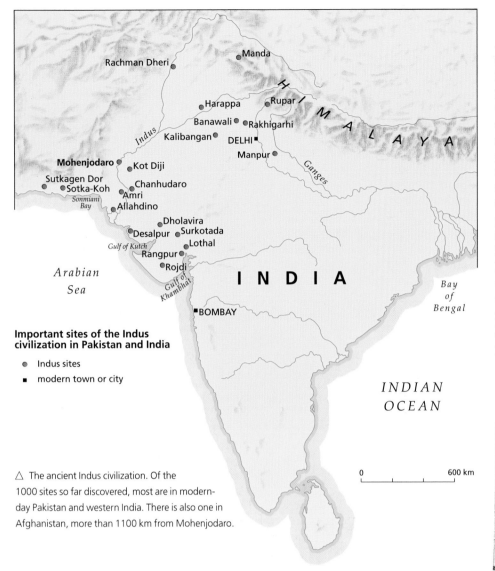

Important sites of the Indus
civilization in Pakistan and India

- Indus sites
- modern town or city

△ The ancient Indus civilization. Of the
1000 sites so far discovered, most are in modern-
day Pakistan and western India. There is also one in
Afghanistan, more than 1100 km from Mohenjodaro.

The Indus language

Although archaeologists have discovered much about the Indus civilization, its language, which has not yet been deciphered, remains a mystery. More than 4000 inscriptions have been found, most of them on small, square seals. These are made of soapstone, engraved with pictures and writing, which were used to make a stamp on soft clay. The inscriptions are usually short and it is thought that they must be the names of goods and people. During recent excavations at the site of Dholavira in western India an inscription of gypsum characters on a large piece of wood was uncovered near the entrance to the site. It is quite possibly the name of the Indus town. Some specialists believe that the writing is related to a Dravidian language that is spoken in parts of southern India today.

△ More than 2500 soapstone Indus seals have
been found. Most have an animal and some writing
engraved on them. These seals from Mohenjodaro
date from between 2500 and 2000 BC. One shows a
hump-backed bull, the other a horse.

The Indus civilization

Mohenjodaro is one of the most important settlements of what archaeologists call the 'Indus civilization'. Over 4000 years ago the Indus was a powerful and highly organized state. So far, almost 1000 Indus sites have been discovered.

The Indus civilization was lost to us for thousands of years. It was only at the beginning of the 20th century that archaeologists recognized the ruined mounds of Harappa (another important Indus city) and Mohenjodaro as part of an ancient state. This state is known by two names: 'Indus' after the River Indus next to which Mohenjodaro was built, and 'Harappan' after the first site to be discovered near the modern town of Harappa. Today Indus settlements look like small hills in the landscape. These mounds, like the tells

of the Middle East, which have formed over thousands of years from the rubble of mudbricks used for buildings.

Most Indus settlements were built according to a uniform pattern. They had the same type of large and small buildings and a sophisticated system of drains, baths and toilets. Mohenjodaro is similar to Harappa, which is 643 km to the northeast, and to Lothal, a trading port about the same distance away to the south. The types of objects found throughout the vast area covered by the state are almost identical, and the organization of trade was the same everywhere.

Excavations on Indus sites began in the 1920s and have continued until the present day. It is impossible to excavate entire large cities – Mohenjodaro and Harappa covered more than 2.5 sq km – so only parts have been excavated.

MOHENJODARO

Today work at Mohenjodaro is concerned with conserving the buildings excavated in previous campaigns. Archaeologists are also trying to solve questions arising from conflicting interpretations on the development of the city. Some specialists believe that the city was devastated by floods on two or three different occasions. They point to layers of river mud and the remains of river shellfish that have been found in some levels of the city.

A team of German and Italian excavators presently working at Mohenjodaro suggest that this mud, and the shellfish found in it, was not deposited there by flooding but dug from outside the city and used to fill gaps in the brickwork. They also claim that floods could never have risen as high as some of the mud layers.

Despite the problems of different interpretation, excavations at Mohenjodaro give us a fairly good idea of what an Indus city was like. Excavations of many other Indus settlements, such as Kalibangan, Lothal and Dholavira, have added to our understanding of the Indus state. However, much is still shrouded in mystery. One day we hope the writing will be deciphered, enabling specialists to translate the inscriptions. Then archaeologists will be able to fit more parts of the Indus puzzle together.

The Citadel and the Lower City

There are two vast mounds at Mohenjodaro, one higher than the other. The highest mound is called the 'Stupa Mound' because of a Buddhist shrine which was built on top of it in the 2nd century AD. The early excavators called this mound the 'Citadel' because it is covered with the remains of monumental buildings. They called the lower mound, which had been the residential area of the city, the 'Lower City'.

Both the Citadel and the Lower City are built on platforms of mudbricks and earth. The buildings on the Citadel mound are on a platform which rose about 13 m above the surrounding plain. Many metres of the site lie buried beneath the water table, which has slowly risen over the millennia. Some archaeologists believe that these platforms were constructed to protect the city from the heavy floods of the Indus River. Others disagree. They point out that the platform of the Citadel is higher than that of the Lower City. This, they say, was deliberately planned in order to impress the people of the Lower City with the importance of the activities which were conducted in the Citadel. Perhaps both interpretations hold a little of the truth.

The Citadel buildings

A number of impressive buildings, which have been given names such as the 'Great Bath', the 'Granary', the 'College' and the 'Assembly Hall', were constructed on the Citadel platform. These were probably government buildings and must have included the building where the city ruler and his attendants lived.

One of the great problems for archaeologists when trying to determine what the large Indus buildings were is to identify the palace and temples. In Egypt and Sumer the decoration of some buildings and rich artefacts found inside them make it easy for us to guess what they were. Although the buildings in the citadel area of Indus cities are immensely impressive,

◁ The Citadel mound, the higher of the two vast mounds at Mohenjodaro. It is called the Citadel because it is covered with the remains of monumental buildings. In the 2nd century AD a Buddhist shrine was built on top of it.

they are undecorated and were not full of luxurious goods. In Egyptian and Sumerian sites, written records sometimes help archaeologists to recognize special buildings. Undoubtedly the Indus script holds the key to the meaning of the large buildings in Indus cities.

The Great Bath

One of the most impressive buildings in the Citadel at Mohenjodaro is the Great Bath, which is rather like a swimming pool in the centre of a courtyard. The pool was surrounded by a pillared verandah behind which were a number of small rooms. A staircase from one of the rooms led to an upper level which no longer exists. Water entered the Bath from a well in one of the rooms and drained away through a large brick drain. At one end of the Bath there is a block of eight small bathrooms divided by a passage. Small drains in each bathroom connected with a larger drain which ran along the middle of the passage. Everything is made with baked bricks.

We do not know what the Great Bath was used for. It was certainly not a

MUDBRICKS

One of the striking features of Mohenjodaro, and of most Indus settlements, is the use of baked mudbricks for construction. The use of mudbricks, whether dried in the sun or baked over fires, is not unusual in itself. What is remarkable at Mohenjodaro is the numbers of baked bricks which were used — literally millions. Where did the clay come from to make the bricks?

When the city was occupied over 4000 years ago the River Indus flowed nearby. Since then, the river has changed its course and now flows over 3 km away. Each spring melting snow from the mountains to the north causes the river to rise and flood its banks, covering a wide area with a layer of fertile mud. Later in the summer, monsoon rains again cause the river to flood. These floods provided the people not only with extremely good land in which to grow their crops but also with the material to make mudbricks. They just had to dig it out of the ground outside the city walls. Even today, this practice continues in parts of Pakistan, India and North Africa. The picture below shows mudbricks being made in Morocco.

When we consider the baked bricks used by the Indus people we must take into account the tons of mud used and the fuel (trees) required to fire them. We must also keep in mind the organization needed to direct the massive brick-making activities and the manpower needed to accomplish all of this.

---

communal swimming pool. Some archaeologists believe that it may have been a place where ritual bathing occurred. This could be true as we know that ritual bathing, before worship in a temple, was considered important in later periods in both India and Pakistan.

The Granary

The Granary is another huge building near the Great Bath. It consists of blocks of bricks about 1.5 m high separated by narrow passages. Sir Mortimer Wheeler, an English archaeologist who excavated the Granary in 1950, thought that a wooden structure had been built on top of these blocks to store grain. The blocks then allowed air to pass through under the grain. He suggested that a mudbrick platform at one end could have been used for lifting and lowering bags of

grain. At the moment we cannot be sure that this interpretation is correct.

Similar buildings have been found in other Indus cities. Archaeologists believe that grain, and perhaps other goods, were stored in these granaries and given to workers as wages. Grain may also have been traded with other towns, cities or countries in exchange for goods the Indus people needed. The granaries look very forbidding, almost like fortresses with their huge mudbrick walls. Some archaeologists believe this shows that the rulers were very powerful and controlled their subjects strictly.

The Lower City

The Lower City, or residential area, is vastly different to the Citadel and spreads over an area of about 2.5 sq km. Today it looks like a number of small mounds,

△ The Great Bath, one of the most impressive buildings on the Citadel. Archaeologists still do not know what it was for. Some believe it was used for ritual bathing, perhaps before worship in a temple, a custom followed in later Indian religions.

▷ Sir Mortimer Wheeler's suggested reconstruction of the Granary, another huge building on the Citadel mound. Archaeologists today are not sure if his interpretation is correct.

◁ The Indus cities had highly sophisticated drainage systems. Brick drains in the houses connected with drains in the street. They were covered by large stone slabs or bricks.

▷ This bronze dancing girl is one of the most famous of the many artefacts that were discovered at Mohenjodaro.

some of which have been partially excavated. It is set out in rectangular blocks with streets running from north to south and east to west. Narrow lanes run off the wide main streets. The streets and lanes are unpaved and some still have the grooves made by the heavy carts that travelled along them.

There are hundreds of one- and two-storey baked brick houses in the residential area. They are usually built around a courtyard and entered from small alleys. The windowless back walls of the houses line the main streets, causing them to look very dull and dreary. Most houses have a bathroom and some have a toilet. City wells provided water, although some houses had private wells. Brick drains in the houses connect with street drains covered with large stone slabs or bricks. Part of the residential area consists of much smaller dwellings where the poorer people may have lived. These are in a block with small two-room units.

A manufacturing area has been uncovered in the Lower City. The artefacts found in the workshops show that people made pottery, metal objects, seals, beads and shell ornaments. In the potters' workshops, for example, excavations have revealed many painted pots decorated with animal

△ A storage pot, one of the many found in the workshop area of the Lower City. Water jars, cooking bowls and drinking cups were also found.

figures. Pots were made on a potter's wheel and fired in large kilns. Potters also produced huge storage jars, water jars, cooking bowls and drinking cups, which would have been used every day.

Metal workers produced simple copper tools: axes, chisels, knives, spearheads and arrowheads, fishhooks and razors. Specialists made copper vases, small bronze animals and figurines as well as exquisite gold and silver jewellery.

Skilled seal makers made the tiny but distinctive Indus seals from blocks of soapstone. The seals were carefully engraved and heated to harden the stone. More than 1000 seals were found at Mohenjodaro.

The Indus people were skilled at making beads of all shapes and sizes from semi-precious stones. Indus beads found on Sumerian sites provide us with evidence for long-distance trade. Shells, which probably came from the coast, were used to make beads and bracelets and to decorate other objects.

▽ Baked clay model of oxen and cart. Tracks made by carts were found during excavations at many Indus sites. The Indus people made many clay figurines. We do not know if they were toys or if they had some religious significance.

suggest that it was important. The number of levels of the site shows it was inhabited for a long time. But we know nothing of its rulers, priests or important citizens. In Egypt and Sumer burials filled with rich goods indicate powerful and important persons. Although Indus burials have been found, none includes the lavish grave goods we might expect to find in a royal grave. Because of the size of the Indus state and the uniformity of settlement patterns, types of tools, pottery, figurines and seals, we believe that the rulers must have exercised a firm control over the country. But the Indus jealously guards many more secrets than do its counterparts in Sumer and Egypt, not least its language. It is an exciting area for archaeologists.

Farming

The regular flooding of the Indus River deposited layers of mud on the surrounding land. Over the years this caused the level of the land to raise. Today those early fields lie well below the modern land surface, but at Kalibangan one field has been found.

How do we know what crops were grown in Indus times and what animals were around? Animal bones and plant remains found in different sites are one source of information. Fragments of clay and pottery have impressions of cereals and textiles. These indicate that wheat, barley and cotton were grown, and that cloth was manufactured from the cotton. Another source of information is seals, which often show animals. The Indus people also made many small baked clay figurines of animals, people and carts. Some of these may have been toys, some may have had a religious meaning. These different lines of evidence show that the animals of Indus times were similar to those that can be found in the area today: sheep, goats, humped-back cattle, flat-backed cattle and buffalo. In addition many wild animals roamed the area, including gazelle, rhinoceros and elephant.

Remaining mysteries

We do not know if Mohenjodaro was the capital city of the Indus state. It is one of the largest early cities known to us. The impressive buildings in the Citadel area

▷ This modern-day ox-cart is similar to the Indus models. Some of the farming methods used by the ancient Indus farmers are still current in the Indus Valley today.

OVERSEAS TRADE

Archaeological excavations in the last 70 years have given us more than a glimpse of the Indus state. Sites on the coast and in Afghanistan in the north have been interpreted as trading posts, suggesting the importance of trade for the Indus civilization. The map opposite shows early trade routes in the region. The Indus people imported different types of wood and stone as well as semi-precious stones and metals. They must have traded for these goods by exporting goods they made. We do not know for certain what these were but they may have been perishable goods such as cotton, woollen cloth and cereals, as well as valuable stone beads. There is evidence for Indus trade in Sumer: distinctive Indus seals and beads have been found on Sumerian sites. Additionally, literary evidence from Sumerian texts speaks of ships laden with goods bound for Sumer sailing from a place called Meluhha, which is believed to refer to the Indus state.

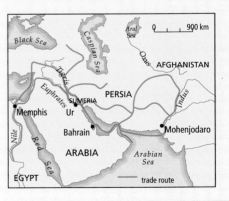

LIFE IN ANCIENT EGYPT

Early Egyptian life sometimes seems surrounded by mystery with its mummies, huge pyramids, colossal monuments and hieroglyphic writing. But it is these tombs, monuments and hieroglyphs that have provided much of the evidence which has allowed us to solve at least part of the mystery of ancient Egypt.

We are incredibly lucky that the ancient Egyptians painted tomb walls with scenes of their life in this world and the life they believed came after death. Fortunately for us, too, they placed objects in the tombs which they felt might be useful to the dead person in the afterlife. Such objects included food, clothes, furniture, tools and dishes. In addition, small wooden or clay models of daily activities, such as making bread or beer, were sometimes placed in the tombs.

A further stroke of immense good luck for us is the dryness of the Egyptian climate, especially inside the tombs. Wooden artefacts, baskets, clothes, food and documents written on papyrus (paper made from the papyrus plant), which would have disintegrated in more humid climates, have been preserved in these conditions. As a result, the tombs and their contents are an invaluable source of information on ancient Egyptian life.

Early explorers

During the 19th century people became very interested in antiquities from ancient cultures. Egyptian artefacts were highly prized and desired for both private and museum collections. Travellers and explorers often removed the more spectacular objects from tombs, without noting their context or position. Large statues from temples were also highly prized, but these could not always be removed.

Enter archaeology

Towards the end of the 19th century archaeological excavations began to play an important part in the recovery and recording of ancient Egyptian life. In 1884 an Englishman, William Flinders Petrie, arrived in Egypt. It was Petrie who laid the foundations for the recovery and recording techniques that are used by archaeologists today, not only in Egypt but also elsewhere in the world.

Before Petrie, excavations in Egypt had concentrated on the large monuments. The smaller objects and their context were ignored. Petrie was interested in the small finds such as potsherds (pieces of broken pottery), amulets (lucky charms), broken flints and so on. He noted their exact position in the ground and was therefore able to relate objects to different occupation levels. (An archaeological site often consists of separate layers of deposits left by the different groups of people who occupied the site over the years.) He carefully studied the shapes of artefacts such as weapons, pottery and stone vessels, which he found at different levels in his excavations. As a result he was able to distinguish the most common types of artefact associated with each occupation layer. Archaeologists call this technique 'typology' and still use it as a basis for relative dating (see page 24).

Ancient historians

Contemporary accounts, written by people who were alive at the time, provide us with another vitally important source of information about ancient Egypt. A Greek man called Herodotus travelled widely in Egypt in 450 BC. He described what he saw and wrote the first history of the country as it was told to him by the Egyptians themselves. The writings of Herodotus are a great gift as they give us first-hand knowledge of the lives, customs and beliefs of people of this early civilization.

The ancient Egyptians themselves have provided us with a detailed written record on all aspects of their life. Manetho, a priest who lived in the 3rd century BC, was the first Egyptian to write a history of his own country. His history, with its list of Pharaohs and the dates of their dynasties, is still used by today's Egyptologists (people who study ancient Egypt).

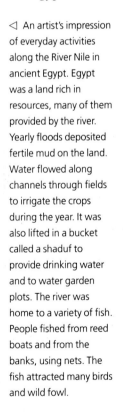

◁ An artist's impression of everyday activities along the River Nile in ancient Egypt. Egypt was a land rich in resources, many of them provided by the river. Yearly floods deposited fertile mud on the land. Water flowed along channels through fields to irrigate the crops during the year. It was also lifted in a bucket called a shaduf to provide drinking water and to water garden plots. The river was home to a variety of fish. People fished from reed boats and from the banks, using nets. The fish attracted many birds and wild fowl.

ANCIENT EGYPTIAN WRITING

Three types of writing were used in ancient Egypt: hieroglyphic, hieratic and demotic. Hieroglyphic writing, invented about 3000 BC, is the earliest writing in Egypt. It is in the form of pictures or pictograms and was used for religious texts. Hieratic writing is a simplified, cursive (joined-up) form of hieroglyphs and was used in legal and business documents. Demotic writing, another type of cursive script, developed around 600 BC. It was then used for everyday purposes while hieroglyphic and hieratic scripts were used for religious texts.

The only problem with Egyptian writing – a problem which lasted for almost 2000 years – was that until the beginning of the 19th century no one could understand it.

The Rosetta Stone

In 1799 a large, black basalt stone was found at Rosetta near Alexandria in Egypt. It was inscribed in three scripts: hieroglyphic, demotic and Greek. This stone, called the Rosetta Stone, proved to be one of the most important finds for Egyptologists because it held the key to understanding hieroglyphic writing. By comparing the Greek and the hieroglyphs, a Frenchman, J. F. Champollion, finally succeeded in solving the mystery of hieroglyphs in 1822. The subsequent translation of written records has provided us with a vast amount of information on ancient Egypt.

△ The Rosetta Stone, with a decree of the Pharaoh Ptolemy V (196 BC) inscribed in three languages: hieroglyphs, demotic and Greek. The Egyptian scripts were finally deciphered 25 years after the stone was discovered.

How the ordinary people lived

There are, then, many different types of evidence which archaeologists use to piece together the story of ancient Egypt: large monuments, tombs (including the pyramids) and their contents, paintings on tomb walls, written documents and inscriptions. The monuments are usually temples or palaces, which give us information about the Pharaoh and his court. But they do not tell us much about the ordinary people and how they lived.

Fortunately wall paintings, artefacts and written sources can help us find some of the answers to this question. Paintings and models show bakeries, breweries, stone working, metal and wood working, jewellery making and building. Just about everything the Egyptians did is recorded in this way. We can also learn a great deal from their villages, some of which have been discovered and excavated.

FOOD PRODUCTION IN ANCIENT EGYPT

Egypt is often called 'the gift of the Nile'. The River Nile rises far to the south of Egypt, close to the equator. In ancient times yearly rains in the south caused the Nile to overflow its banks and flood the surrounding land, leaving a layer of rich, black mud. This mud fertilized the land, making it good for farming. The ancient Egyptians called the fertile land 'the Black Land' because of the colour of the mud. They directed the flood waters into irrigation channels to water their crops.

Immediately beyond the fertile strip, the desert starts so abruptly that in places it is almost possible to stand with one foot on desert and one foot on farmland. Without the life-giving waters of the Nile, all of Egypt would be desert. The ancient Egyptians called the desert 'the Red Land' because of the colour of the sand and rocks. The Black Land was a place of life, growth and safety, but the Red Land was a place of death and horror.

Despite its desert areas, Egypt was a land of plenty. As well as a variety of food, the land provided the stone necessary to build temples and carve statues; semi-precious stones such as carnelian and turquoise; and, most importantly, gold.

The agricultural cycle

Emmer wheat, barley and flax were the most common crops in ancient Egypt. Bread and beer were made from wheat and barley, and linen cloth from flax. We can discover much about the production of food from wall paintings, models, artefacts and written sources.

Planting took place in October and November after the Nile flood waters had receded. Wall paintings show farmers ploughing the ground, using either a hand plough or one drawn by cows, in preparation for planting the seeds. Numerous wooden ploughs, hoes (also used to prepare the ground) and baskets (to hold the seeds) have been found in excavations throughout Egypt. There are also models of farmers, sometimes with a helper, and the ploughing team.

▷ A wooden model of a ploughing scene. Models such as this, which were placed in tombs, show us how ancient Egyptians lived and worked.

▷ A view of the Nile today. The green, fertile strip of land by the banks of the river ends abruptly where the desert begins. In ancient times the Nile was not only a source of food but the main means of transport between villages and towns. The river also provided an important link between African countries and goods to the south and the Mediterranean world to the north.

Harvesting the crops

Miriam Stead, formerly of the British Museum, has explained a harvest scene (see above) painted on the tomb of Menna at Thebes, the sacred city of ancient Egypt. In the picture Menna (bottom left), sitting under a shade, watches his workers cut the grain with sickles (curved pieces of wood fitted with sharp pieces of flint). A girl follows them, picking up the grain that falls on to the ground. At this stage only the top part of the stalk (called the ears of grain) is harvested. Later the bottom part, the straw, will be pulled up. A harvester quenches his thirst (probably with beer) from a jar which a young girl has given him. It is her job to see that the workers do not get too thirsty. In the background a woman sits under a tree with her baby. She has the workers' lunch in a bowl in front of her.

We know, from another tomb painting, that sometimes a flautist played music while the men worked, perhaps to make the work less boring.

As the scene progresses to the right of the picture a large basket of grain is carried away on poles by two men. Children collect the grain that drops out of the basket. Two children fight over who gets the grain.

Threshing and winnowing

The painting then shows two men using large forks to prepare the ears of grain for threshing. This is to separate the grain from the surrounding case (the husk). A worker drives cattle over the grain to thresh it (top right), while other men use their forks to help the process. The grain is then winnowed to remove any remaining chaff. Men pick up the grain in flat wooden spoons called winnowing fans and throw it in the air. The wind then carries away the husks while the seed falls to the ground. Finally, the size of the harvest is recorded by the scribes, who take away a certain amount of grain to pay taxes and rent. (In ancient Egypt many people could not write. Scribes were specially trained in writing, and would have done jobs involving writing and the recording of information.)

The grain was stored in granaries and then paid as wages to workers. Money as we know it did not exist; instead people traded goods and work.

Artefacts such as sickles, wooden winnowing fans, jars, baskets, musical flutes and models of granaries show that the painted scenes were true to life.

◁▽ Agricultural tools: a sickle (below) with flint blades and a wooden winnowing fan (left). Both can be seen in use in the harvest scene above.

The Egyptian diet

Bread made from the wheat and beer made from the barley were the most important parts of the Egyptian diet. Numerous paintings, sketches and models of people baking or brewing have come from tombs. The actual grinding stones, cooking pots and other objects used in food preparation and cooking have been found both in tombs and on settlement sites. In addition there are written accounts of the food given to workers. Herodotus tells us that workers often had radishes and onions for lunch; a temple scene on a wall at Karnak (a village in the south of Egypt near Aswan) shows a workman eating his lunch of bread, cucumber and onion.

△ Harvest scene painted in the tomb of a nobleman, Menna, at Thebes. Scenes of everyday life were often painted on tomb walls.

Some of the food, placed with the mummies, has been preserved: bread, nuts, meat, fish, fruit and so on. The banquet scenes painted on tomb walls show that the ancient Egyptians were people who delighted in food.

▷ A wooden model showing Egyptians killing a cow, brewing beer, carrying water, grinding grain, and cooking bread in two ovens.

THE WORKMEN'S VILLAGE OF DEIR EL-MEDINEH

It took many years to build tombs for the Pharaoh and his queen. Construction often began as soon as the new Pharaoh succeeded to the throne. Tombs were not built in the city where the Pharaoh had his court, but usually some distance away. During most of the 18th and 20th dynasties of the New Kingdom (about 1540–1070 BC), the capital of Egypt was at Thebes. The tombs of the Theban Pharaohs were built across the river from Thebes on the edge of the desert, in the area known as the Valley of the Kings and the Valley of the Queens. Groups of workmen were constantly employed to work on the tombs; they lived in villages close to their work. One such village is Deir el-Medineh.

Deir el-Medineh is not as well preserved nor as spectacular as the monuments and temples of the cities. This is because it is made mainly from sun-dried mudbricks, which collapse after a time, whereas the important monuments in the cities are made of stone. Parts of the village were excavated in the 19th century and the early 20th century by Italian and German archaeologists. In the early 1920s a team of French archaeologists began systematic excavations which continued, with some breaks, until the 1970s.

▷ Remains of the mudbrick village of Deir el-Medineh, built to house the men who worked on the royal tombs.

Evidence revealed by excavations

The French excavations uncovered a wealth of documentary evidence about the community, written on papyrus, stelae (stone slabs with inscriptions) and ostraca (broken pieces of pottery or stone on which people wrote). Thousands of fragments of ostraca were found in a pit outside the town walls. This was probably one of the rubbish dumps used by the villagers.

The Egyptian scribes at the royal tombs kept careful accounts of everything that happened in the village and at the work site. These were inscribed on ostraca or written on papyrus. They record the type of work done, how it was done, tools distributed to the workmen, payment of wages, judgement of disputes, festival days and so on. These accounts, together with the artefacts, the paintings and the remains of the houses, provide us with a detailed picture of life in Deir el-Medineh.

Ancient Egypt, then, is not as mysterious as we once thought; the Egyptians left us many clues about their everyday lives.

The building of the village

Deir el-Medineh, founded around 1500 BC, was occupied for about 450 years, from the 18th to the 21st dynasties. Built on the edge of the desert, it was linked to Thebes by a single road. The mudbricks of the thick wall surrounding the village are stamped with the name of King Tuthmosis I, the first Pharaoh to be buried in the Valley of the Kings. We know then that the wall was constructed during his reign near the beginning of the 18th dynasty. Perhaps the isolation of the village and its enclosing wall were deliberately planned by the authorities to enable them to keep an eye on the workmen and protect the secrets of the royal tomb. Indeed, the workmen stayed in small huts much closer to the tombs while they were working, only returning to the village on their days off.

The layout of the village

Excavations at Deir el-Medineh revealed the layout of the village and its houses. A street, going from north to south, divided the village into two. At its largest (in the

19th dynasty, about 1300–1200 BC) there were 70 houses inside the village. The terraced houses were arranged in blocks with one entrance facing the main street. As the village grew, 50 more houses were built outside the north wall.

The nearest source of water was the river, roughly 1.6 km away. Excavation shows that water was brought in special containers and placed in a large storage tank outside the north gate. From here it was collected by villagers and stored in large pots, which have been found near the houses.

The workmen of Deir el-Medineh

The scribes' accounts provide detailed evidence on the organization of the workmen. Documents refer to two groups of workers called 'gangs'. These were divided into a right and a left gang, probably those who worked on the right and the left side of the tomb. Each gang consisted of about 60 workmen. A foreman and a deputy helped them, saw that the work was done according to the architect's plan, and settled arguments between the workers. Every day the scribe wrote down who was absent from work and why. He also noted how work was progressing and anything of importance that had happened during the day. His reports were given to the Pharaoh's representative, who visited the site occasionally.

The work day was eight hours long. There was no work on the 10th, 20th or 30th day of the month, nor on festival days. Workers were given copper tools to work with. Baked clay lamps, with wicks made of old rags and filled with vegetable oil, lit up the interior of the tomb.

The workmen were paid wages of bread and barley, as well as fish, vegetables, fats, oils and clothing. At times, when the workmen did not get their payments on time, they went on strike, only returning to work when they received their wages. These are the first known strikes.

The documents from Deir el-Medineh reveal many more fascinating facts about the working life of the tomb labourers and their life with their families at home in the village. They were not slaves, as some people used to think; they lived well.

At first houses were made of mudbricks, but later basements and parts of the walls were made of stone, painted white or decorated with paintings. Columns, doors and windows were often painted blue or yellow.

Plans of house remains show that the average house had four rooms, usually placed one behind the other. Artefacts found inside the houses have helped archaeologists reconstruct the probable function of each room. The entrance room generally contained a large, boxlike, brick construction (perhaps a shrine or bed) as well as spaces for offerings and paintings of gods, in particular the household god Bes. The room may have functioned as a household shrine room as well as a reception area. The living room, behind the entrance hall, had a high ceiling supported by columns. It usually included a small brick structure – perhaps a bed or a table – and small windows. Two smaller rooms behind the living room would have served as bedrooms and storage areas.

Some houses also had one or two cellars used for storage. The kitchen, at the back of the house, was a small walled courtyard with a pottery or brick oven, pots for storing grain and a stone for grinding it.

The roof, which could be reached by a staircase from one of the rooms, was made of wooden beams and straw matting, some of which was uncovered during excavation. Small holes in the matting allowed light to pass through to the rooms below.

◁ An ostraca written in hieratic. It is a list of 40 workmen showing the days they were absent from work (in black) and the reasons for their absence (in red). Reasons include 'illness' and 'stung by a scorpion'.

THE ANCIENT OLYMPIC GAMES

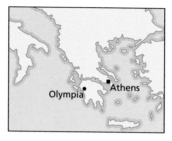

The decline of the Olympic site began in AD 395 when the Games were abandoned on Roman imperial command. Invaders plundered many of the buildings and shrines between the 5th and 8th centuries AD. Earthquakes, floods and landslides covered the site with over 4 m of debris and river sediments. Olympia lay hidden and forgotten for centuries. It was not until 1766 that it was rediscovered by Richard Chandler, an English antiquarian. French archaeologists began excavations in 1829, but it was a later German team that uncovered much of the ancient Olympic complex.

The first Olympic Games were held in 776 BC, at Olympia in Greece. For the next 1000 years the Games were held every four years. The Olympic site was then lost to us for a further 1000 years. Its rediscovery in 1766 and subsequent excavations have told us much about the ancient Games.

The modern Olympic Games

The first modern Olympic Games were held in 1896 in Athens. Every four years, athletes from throughout the world gather together to test their athletic prowess. They have spent years of hard training in preparation for this prestigious event. An Olympic gold medal signifies supreme excellence in their sport. The pride victors feel as they stand on the podium is shared by spectators in the stands, particularly their fellow country people, and by millions of television viewers worldwide. On their return home, victorious athletes are joyfully welcomed and fêted. Sometimes they receive special honours from their country. Fame and fortune often, but not always, follow Olympic success, today as well as in the past.

△ Linford Christie of Great Britain wins the 100 m sprint at the Olympic Games in Barcelona, 1992.

◁ Among the many important buildings at Olympia around 100 BC were:
1 Temple of Zeus **2** Temple of Hera **3** Leonidaion Hotel **4** Workshop of Pheidias **5** Palaestra **6** Gymnasium **7** Stadium **8** Hippodrome or horse-track

SOURCES OF INFORMATION

Archaeologists have uncovered the material remains of the Games from the site itself. These include foundations and parts of buildings, statues, race tracks, artefacts in iron, bronze, terracotta and clay. Further information comes from artefacts found in other sites of the Greek and Roman world whose athletes competed in the Games. Written descriptions of events and victory songs have added to our understanding of the prestigious event.

Commemorative statues and coins

Successful athletes or their sponsors sometimes commemorated victories by having bronze or marble statues made and erected at Olympia, and often in their home towns too. Most statues have

▷ Philip of Macedon, father of Alexander the Great, had this gold coin minted to celebrate the victory of his chariot team in the Olympic Games in 356 BC.

Decorated vases

A large body of detailed information comes from decorated vases. All aspects of the Olympic Games are well represented: preparation, competition, judging, prize-giving, celebration and religious rites. The vases are illustrated in such detail that it is possible to reconstruct specific techniques of a sport, such as the long jump or the short-distance and long-distance foot (running) races.

Written records

Much was written about the Olympic Games. The best and most vivid descriptions are by Pausanias, who wrote a travel guide to Greece in the 2nd century AD. At first no systematic records were kept of the Olympics, but later lists of winners were published by individual writers. Eventually Olympia began to keep its own records. Unfortunately, these have not survived. However, the information recorded by ancient writers based on these lost lists has enabled modern researchers to compile a partial list of Olympic victors.

Other literary sources

At times the richer champions commissioned poems or songs to commemorate

been lost or broken. Sometimes the bronze and marble was later used for other purposes. However, the Romans made replicas of statues (the most famous is that of a discus-thrower). Not only do these show particular events, but they throw light on technical aspects of those events.

Although many statues have disappeared, the bases on which they stood often remain. These are important because they provide details such as the victor's name and country, and the type of competition. In the 2nd century BC the rules and names of the supervising officials were usually inscribed on the bases.

Some states had coins minted to celebrate Olympic successes. Among the most famous are those of Philip II of Macedon, father of Alexander the Great, who also had a circular building (the Philippeion) erected to commemorate his victories.

◁ The Temple of Hera, built around 600 BC, is the oldest building at Olympia. Women were forbidden to compete in the Olympic Games, but they had their own games in honour of Hera.

their victories. The Greek poet, Pindar, was eagerly sought after and wrote many such odes. One was about Hiero of Syracuse who had been victorious in a horse race. At least 45 of Pindar's odes still survive.

The fame and prowess of some athletes spread far and wide and the stories about them became more exaggerated over time. Eventually they became heroes of legend. Such was the case with Milo of Croton, a famous wrestler.

THE BUILDINGS AT OLYMPIA

A detailed plan of the site shows that the number of buildings and sports areas increased during the period Olympia was used for the Games. Excavations have also revealed how some sports areas, for example the stadium, changed their location within the site over time. Today at Olympia we see the ruins of the once great complex.

The original Olympic Games were held to honour the greatest god of Greek mythology, Zeus. They were a combination of religious rites and sporting events. The most sacred sanctuary to Zeus, and the central area of Olympia, was the Altis. Although it was just a grove during the first years of the Games, gradually it became filled with temples,

▷ Head of the Greek god Apollo presiding over a mythological battle. The scene is sculpted on one end of the Temple of Zeus at Olympia. Apollo was the son of Zeus in whose honour the Olympic Games were held.

ARCHAEOLOGICAL EXCAVATIONS

Archaeology has clarified some of the information passed to us from literary sources. In turn, these writings have helped archaeologists understand some aspects of their finds which might otherwise have remained a mystery. The first small-scale excavations were conducted by French archaeologists in 1829.

Some 46 years later a German team began excavations on a larger scale. They removed the debris covering most of the Altis, the main sanctuary area, and uncovered some of the statues from the Temple of Zeus. The work was well documented, and finds were carefully recorded. Sculptures were drawn and attempts were made to date the construction of each building by studying architectural styles and

construction methods. Eventually pottery became a useful chronological indicator. The archaeologists' reports are still useful references for modern-day researchers.

The Germans continued excavating at Olympia in the 20th century. They have unearthed thousands of artefacts and uncovered the remains of many buildings and features. Their excavations have allowed them to reconstruct the athletic stadium as it was in the 4th century BC. They also discovered debris from the workshop of Pheidias, a famous sculptor at Olympia. This includes clay moulds, fragments of ivory, glass ornaments, bronze and bone tools, and a clay cup inscribed with the words 'I belong to Pheidias'.

cult places and statues erected to honour Zeus. Nothing remains of the Great Altar of Zeus, the sacrificial altar located in the Altis, but we know of it from Pausanias.

The Temple of Zeus

The Temple of Zeus is the principal temple in the Altis. A gold shield dedicated to Zeus indicates that the temple, completed in 456 BC, took ten years to build. It survived for about 1000 years before it was first damaged by fire and then demolished by an earthquake.

The temple was an enormous multi-pillared building with a white marble roof. Many statues adorned the temple, the most impressive being the huge, richly decorated statue of Zeus made by Pheidias. Nothing remains of this statue today but again we know of it from Pausanias' description.

The Gymnasium and the Palaestra

Two buildings, the Gymnasium and the Palaestra, dominate the western area of Olympia. These were places where the athletes could practise. A race track as long as that in the stadium, with starting blocks at each end, was found in the Gymnasium. Many athletes could practise at one time in the Gymnasium.

The Palaestra consists of a smaller, square colonnade surrounding a courtyard. Here boxers, wrestlers and long jumpers practised. Among the rooms at the Palaestra were an oiling room where athletes oiled their bodies to protect them from the sun, a powdering room, a rest room and a bathroom. Most of the rooms had benches where athletes or visitors could sit.

Bathing facilities

Excavations have also revealed a number of different types of bathing facilities built at different periods during the Games' history: hip baths, cold and hot baths, steam baths and a swimming pool have all been identified. The existence of bathing facilities at Olympia from an early date indicates the importance of bathing for athletes.

The stadium

Most competitions, except for the horse and chariot races, took place in the stadium. Excavations show that five stadia were built. The one from the 4th century BC has been reconstructed. It was rectangular with banks on each side for the spectators. The track itself was 600 Olympic feet long (192.8 m). At each end of the track there was a row of stone starting blocks with spaces for footholds.

In the earliest Olympics the starting line was scratched in the sand. Some people believe that this is the origin of the saying 'starting from scratch'.

The track was separated from the spectators' banks by small stone blocks. A water channel ran between the stone blocks and the embankment to provide cool drinking water for the spectators. The foundations of the judges' stand have been uncovered on one side of the track. Although no traces of the judges' seats survive, they are illustrated on vases. There were no seats for the spectators.

Competitors and judges entered the stadium from the Altis through a covered passage. The stone-lined walls and archway are still clearly visible. It is easy to imagine the excitement of athletes and spectators alike as processions passed through the tunnel into the stadium.

The hippodrome

Pausanias describes the hippodrome or horse track and the complex set of starting gates, but nothing remains of them. This is not surprising as the track would have been a large grass area without any special buildings, easily destroyed by centuries of flooding.

△ A passageway connected the Altis with the sports stadium. Processions of athletes and judges emerged from the tunnel into a packed stadium to the tumultuous acclaim of the spectators.

▷ The stadium consisted of a rectangular track with grass banks on each side which could accommodate 40,000 to 45,000 spectators. The track was made of clay and lightly covered with sand.

Other buildings

There are many other buildings at Olympia, each with its own special name and function. Some are associated with the religious nature of the site, some are offices, some are connected to sporting aspects, one is the hotel Leonidaion (for important visitors only). Pausanias says that during the Games a banquet was given for athletes at the Prytaneion, the official building of the chief officer of the Games. Fragments of bronze vessels found in the excavations support his account.

THE GAMES

There were far fewer events in the ancient Olympics than in the modern-day Games. They included foot races, wrestling, boxing, the pankration (a combination of wrestling and boxing), the pentathlon (consisting of discus-throwing, long jump, javelin-throwing, running and wrestling, all completed in one afternoon), horse races and chariot races. Evidence for these competitions comes from written accounts, vase paintings and sculptures. Excavation has uncovered some artefacts used in particular sports (for example jumping weights) as well as figurines and statues of athletes, horses and chariots.

△ Competitors in the dolichos or long-distance race. This race covered 20–24 lengths of the stadium.

Pausanias tells us that the Olympic festival lasted five days, but that preparations began a year before. Originally only Greek males could take part in the Games, but as the Romans became powerful, they too participated. No female competitors were permitted; they had their own games in honour of Hera. One month before the beginning of the Games, all the athletes went to the city of Elis, which was 58 km from Olympia. Here they underwent a strict regime of training and diet in preparation for the Games. Two days before the Games started they went in procession to Olympia, by then packed with visitors from all over the Greek world.

Foot races

The stade or short foot race was the most important competition of the Games as each Olympiad was named after the winner of the stade race. The race was one stade long (one length of the stadium). Other races included the diaulos (2 stades) and the long-distance dolichos race covering 20–24 stades. Leonidas of Rhodes was probably the most famous athlete, winning all three events in four successive Olympiads. Like all of the athletes, he ran in the nude.

indicate a slight difference in throwing techniques between ancient and modern athletes. Many scenes show a musician accompanying the event. These facts, and the relatively short distance of the throw (the only recorded distance is 30 m), have led some modern researchers to believe that a smooth, rhythmic style was more important than distance.

The ancient javelins were made of light wood and had a leather strip wound around the middle which the athlete used to direct the javelin. Writers of the time record throwing distances of 91 m. Vase paintings often depict athletes with three javelins, suggesting that they may have been allowed three throws.

The long jump

The long jump was very different from that which we know today. Jumpers held weights called halteres in their hands. Researchers have been able to reconstruct the use of halteres during the jumping sequence from the many scenes on vases. They were swung forward on take off and backward just before land-

ing. Halteres vary in size, weight and shape. The shape changed according to fashion, and has been used to date different periods. Two distances have been recorded for the long jump, both over 16 m. The distance may be the length of two jumps added together.

Wrestling and pankration

Wrestling, boxing and pankration contests were the bloodiest of all events, although wrestling was not nearly as dangerous as either boxing or the pankration. They are all well illustrated on vase paintings. Two types of wrestling occurred, upright or standing and ground. The aim in upright wrestling was to throw the opponent to the ground three times. Ground wrestling continued until one competitor acknowledged defeat by raising his right hand and pointing his index finger. Biting and gouging (digging fingers into the body) were forbidden.

Wrestlers put powder over their oiled bodies so that opponents could get a grip. After the competition they used a long

We know from written accounts that athletes did warm-up exercises before their race, and that those who made false starts were whipped. Vase paintings show that running styles varied according to the race. It is easy to distinguish the speed of sprinters from the more even movements of long-distance runners.

The hoplitodromos or race-in-armour is unknown in the modern Olympics. The competitors wore helmet and greaves (shin protectors) and carried a round shield. Some vase paintings of the hoplitodromos show athletes stooping to pick up shields they have dropped.

Discus and javelin events

Some discuses have survived; most are made of bronze although a few are marble and one is lead. We know that three official discuses were kept at Olympia. One discus found during excavations belonged to Poplius Asclepiades of Corinth, who dedicated it to Zeus after his victory in the pentathlon in AD 241.

Illustrations of discus-throwing on vases and sculptures of discus-throwers

△ Discus-throwers achieved shorter distances than those of today. Vase paintings often show musicians playing while athletes exercise. Perhaps discus-throwers aimed to achieve a smooth, dance-like movement rather than great distance.

▷ A competitor in the long jump is about to land. He swings weights (halteres) backwards in order to propel his body forwards a few more centimetres. A judge supervises the event. The Greeks considered the long jump to be the most difficult event.

curved instrument called a strigil to scrape the oil, powder and sand from their skin.

The pankration was a brutal event which combined boxing and wrestling but it was loved by the crowds. Some vase paintings show pankratists breaking the rules. Writers describe the displeasure of spectators and judges when this occurred.

Boxing

Boxing, too, was a brutal but popular sport. Boxing gloves changed over time. Until 500 BC long strips of soft leather were bound around and attached by loops to the hand, leaving the fingers free. On some vases we see boxers fixing their bindings; others show strips of binding hanging in bundles. Later, much tougher leather strips were wrapped around the boxer's hand and knuckles. Deadliest of all, however, were gloves reinforced with iron and lead pieces, introduced in Roman times.

Contests occurred in the open but we are not sure if they took place in boxing rings. Illustrations show various types of punches aimed mainly at the opponent's head, and the damage inflicted on the boxers' faces.

Horse and chariot races

There were two types of chariot race: one used two horses and the other used four horses. Horse and chariot owners did not usually take part in the equestrian competitions personally, but hired jockeys and charioteers. However, it was the owners who received the victory crown, while the jockey or charioteer was given the winner's ribbon. Chariot owners were particularly keen to win the four-horse chariot race for the great prestige it brought them.

Chariots were usually made of wood, wickerwork and leather and had no springs. From Pausanias we know that the length of the races ranged from 1.6 km to about 13 km. Contestants had to drive their chariots up and down the field, turning around a post at each end. There were certainly many bumps and accidents at the turns. A trumpeter indicated the last half lap, and we can well imagine the excitement as the race reached its climax.

The horse races followed the chariot races on the same course. The field would have been churned up from the chariot races, so the horses often fell and jockeys were often thrown, especially as they rode bareback and without stirrups (saddles and stirrups were not known at that time).

Prize-giving

Victors were crowned with a wreath made from a branch of a sacred olive tree which grew near the Temple of Zeus. Pausanias writes of an ivory and gold table in the Temple of Hera where the victory wreaths were displayed. The winners also wore victory ribbons around their head, arms and legs; later they carried a palm branch.

As well as the main banquet for victors, Pausanias describes many smaller, private celebrations held during the Olympiad when the air rang with music and singing. Songs and poems were often written especially for the occasion.

At the close of the Games spectators and contestants began the journey home. The departure of thousands from Olympia on foot and by boat must have been chaotic.

△ Boxing was a brutal but popular sport. Here the combatants' hands are bound with strips of leather. One of the boxers has suffered a blow to the nose, which is bleeding.

▽ Victors were crowned with a wreath of olive branches. Victors are sometimes shown wearing victory ribbons on their arms and legs and holding a palm branch.

LIFE AND DEATH AT POMPEII

Most evidence of ancient settlements and human activities disappears long before an excavation occurs, as it either disintegrates or is lost over the centuries. Only in rare circumstances do archaeologists find a site preserved very much as it was in antiquity. The city of Pompeii is one such site.

On the morning of 24 August AD 79 Mount Vesuvius erupted, burying the area around the Bay of Naples in Italy under tons of volcanic ash and lava. This was a grim disaster for the Romans but a gift for archaeologists because the eruption sealed and preserved the towns of Pompeii and Herculaneum. Preservation is such that archaeologists have been able to reconstruct the daily life of Pompeii in great detail. Although much was known about the Romans – about their armies, conquests, emperors, and large cities, for example – little was known about the lives of ordinary people in small towns. Excavations at Pompeii have provided this missing information in abundance.

The eruption of Vesuvius

Pliny the Younger was a boy of 17 in AD 79. He lived with his mother and uncle (Pliny the Elder) across the bay from Pompeii. He saw and described the eruption in a letter to Tacitus, a Roman historian. 'A horrible black cloud ripped by sudden bursts of fire, writhing snake-like and revealing sudden flashes larger than lightning... the cloud began to descend upon the earth and cover the sea... and now came the ashes,... an ominous thick smoke, spreading over the earth like a flood.... We were enveloped in night – not a moonless night or one dimmed by cloud, but the darkness of a sealed room without lights.' When normal daylight eventually returned two days later, Pliny tells us that 'everything appeared changed – covered by a thick layer of ashes like an abundant snowfall'.

The fate of Pompeii's inhabitants

Pompeii's terrified inhabitants ran away or took refuge inside houses and in cellars. Some died as buildings collapsed on them, others died of asphyxiation by the poisonous gases emitted from the volcano. In one house 18 people died

△ Mosaics of dogs, such as this one, and skeletons of dogs have been found at Pompeii. One unfortunate dog was strangled by its leash while trying to escape during the eruption.

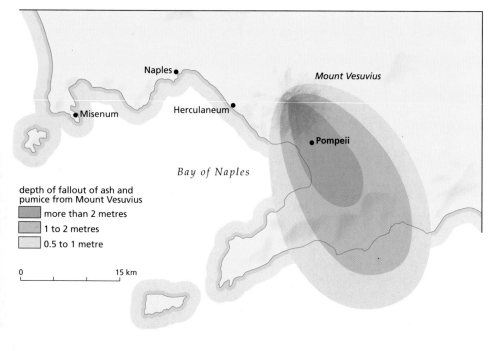

◁ Map of the Bay of Naples showing the area most affected when Mount Vesuvius erupted. Before the volcanic eruption of AD 79 Pompeii, a harbour town, was on the coast. Today it is 2 km inland.

depth of fallout of ash and pumice from Mount Vesuvius
- more than 2 metres
- 1 to 2 metres
- 0.5 to 1 metre

0   15 km

huddled in the cellar, covering their faces in a vain attempt to protect themselves from the fumes. Women with babies and children clasping their parents have been found as they died. Some people tried to hide their valuable possessions or take them with them, but to no avail. One man was found clasping a bronze statue, both crushed under a ceiling which had fallen on top of them.

How the evidence was preserved

How do we know so much about the terror-stricken people of Pompeii? The ash which buried them hardened around the shape of their fully clothed bodies. Although the bodies eventually disintegrated, the shapes, and even details of clothes, were impressed in the ash. Guiseppe Fiorelli, a 19th-century Italian archaeologist at Pompeii, devised a way

of recreating the bodies. He made a small hole in the hardened ash and poured plaster of Paris through it into the space once occupied by the body. When the plaster had dried and hardened he chipped away the surrounding stone to

△ The excavated town of Pompeii, dominated by Mount Vesuvius. Bottom right are the two theatres and left of centre is the Forum.

▽ Cast of the body of a young girl who tried in vain to protect her face from the deadly gases emitted by the volcano.

reveal a perfect plaster cast of the body. This system of making casts has been used for bodies, doors, windows and tree roots. Today, a transparent glass-fibre liquid is used instead of plaster so that bones or artefacts will also be visible.

The early excavations

Pompeii lay buried under 3–5 m of ash and pumice for 1700 years. When first rediscovered the ruins were plundered for treasures to adorn royal palaces and the houses of the rich. By the middle of the 18th century its fame, and that of neighbouring Herculaneum (which had been engulfed in lava), had spread far and wide. Excavations began, although they were poor and rather carelessly planned, and not much more than treasure hunts. The progress of the 18th-century excavations was recorded by visiting artists and writers, who have left us impressions of what they saw. These are of great interest today, as they illustrate the early stages of excavation.

The work of Guiseppe Fiorelli

Under the direction of Guiseppe Fiorelli in 1860, work at Pompeii became more scientific. He cleaned up the rubble left from the old excavations and made a plan of the town. He divided Pompeii into regions and blocks called 'insulae'. Each 'insula' and house was given a number, which archaeologists still use today. He then made a plan to excavate the site systematically, area by area and house by house. Fiorelli kept records detailing the context and position of finds, and progress of the excavations.

Pompeii is full of beautiful wall paintings and mosaics, many of which had been plundered before Fiorelli's time. He insisted, where possible, that they remain in place. He also began to reconstruct some of the buildings, replacing roofs and erecting columns. For the first time, the emphasis was on conservation and preservation of the town. And, of course, he invented his famous method of making plaster casts.

Excavations continued well into the 20th century. Today about four-fifths of Pompeii has been uncovered. Indeed, the excavations of Pompeii are the most complete of any town ever undertaken.

DAILY LIFE IN POMPEII

The joy for archaeologists working at Pompeii is the different lines of evidence available to help them discover what daily life was like. The ash and pumice from the eruption which sealed the town so completely also preserved it. Various areas of the town have been uncovered: streets with large and small houses, gardens, shops, theatres, temples, bath-houses and cemeteries. Thousands of artefacts used daily by the Roman citizens and their slaves were preserved within the buildings: furniture, a variety of boxes, jars and other containers, jewellery and precious goods. Preservation is so good at Pompeii that even food has been found.

The Pompeians painted the walls of their houses with scenes of everyday life – their work, their leisure activities, the gods they worshipped – as well as portraits and purely decorative scenes. Mosaics were another favoured form of decoration; like the wall paintings, they depict life in the town. Writings on the walls tell us about the thoughts, likes and dislikes of the people, what they did and the price of goods. Accounts of writers of the time add

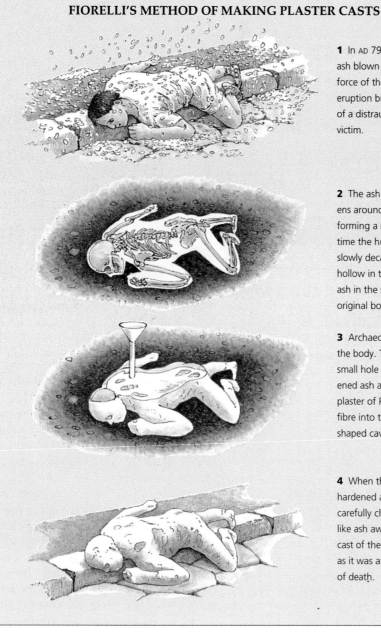

FIORELLI'S METHOD OF MAKING PLASTER CASTS

1 In AD 79 pumice and ash blown out by the force of the volcanic eruption bury the body of a distraught Pompeii victim.

2 The ash slowly hardens around the body, forming a mould. Over time the human remains slowly decay leaving a hollow in the rock-hard ash in the shape of the original body.

3 Archaeologists find the body. They make a small hole in the hardened ash and pour wet plaster of Paris or glass fibre into the body-shaped cavity.

4 When the plaster has hardened archaeologists carefully chip the rock-like ash away to reveal a cast of the body exactly as it was at the moment of death.

▽ The Via del Abbondanza. Shops and businesses along this street included taverns, bars, an iron-monger, a bronzesmith, a laundry and a cloth-making house. Shopkeepers advertised their goods on the walls outside their shops.

to the picture. Through careful study of all this evidence archaeologists have been able to provide us with an amazingly detailed picture of the way people lived in this small Roman town.

The streets of Pompeii

In AD 79 Pompeii was a coastal town. The eruption filled the bay with volcanic deposits so that today it lies 2 km inland. It is surrounded by a wall with eight entrance gates. Inside, wide and narrow streets, some paved with blocks of lava stone, criss-cross the town. Street pavements or sidewalks, made of rubble and mortar with large lava kerbstones, are much higher than the street surface.

The centres of the streets are usually higher than the edges to allow water to drain away. The drainage system at Pompeii was so poor that putrefying rubbish would have collected along the edges of the street; it must have been quite smelly. In places, large stepping stones cross the streets, which would have allowed people to cross without getting their feet dirty. The gaps between the stepping stones were wide enough to allow the wheels of carts to pass through. Grooves made by the constant traffic of cart wheels can still be seen along some streets.

An aqueduct brought water from the nearby hills to water towers in the town. From there it was carried through lead pipes under the pavements to the public baths, wealthy houses and public water fountains. Some pavements have been so worn down by the continuous stream of modern-day tourists that the lead piping is visible, and in danger of breaking up.

Shopkeepers advertised their goods on the walls outside their shops. One boasted: 'Once one of my hams is cooked and set before a customer, before he tastes it, he licks the saucepan in which it was cooked.' Graffiti on tavern walls shows the pleasure or displeasure of customers: 'Health to you Victoria', 'Innkeeper, may you drown in your own sewage-wine'.

Artefacts, wall slogans and wall paintings show us that butchers, potters, bronzesmiths, ironmongers, bakers and leather workers were among the many traders in Pompeii. There were also shops which dealt in luxury goods for those people who could afford them; one wall painting shows cupids as goldsmiths.

◁ All houses in Pompeii had gardens. The House of Vetti had a colonnaded courtyard filled with statues.

▽ A stone counter in one of the bars at Pompeii. Large pottery jars of food fitted into the circular recesses in the counter.

Where people lived

The importance of Pompeii lies in the information it provides about the daily life of ordinary people. It was a busy port town, full of shops, taverns and restaurants, and with large residential areas. The rich lived in enormous houses with many rooms and beautiful gardens, guarded by servants and dogs. The poor often lived in rooms above shops. Small shops usually consisted of two rooms: a back room where the family lived and a front room which opened on to the street and was the shop proper. Similar shops may be seen in Mediterranean towns today. In larger shops the living quarters were often on the first floor.

Shops of all types

Stone counters have been found in food shops and snack bars. These counters have spaces into which large pots of grain, dried food and water or wine could be placed, covered by stone lids. Ovens under some counters were used to heat food and wine. Meats were probably hung from a rod near the entrance. Artefacts uncovered during excavations include baked clay dishes and jugs, bronze pots, kettles, dishes and bronze weighing scales.

FOOD AND DRINK AT POMPEII

It is estimated that Pompeii had about 10,000 – perhaps as many as 20,000 – inhabitants. Luckily food seems to have been plentiful. Although Mount Vesuvius posed a danger, it was also a source of food for the town. Farms and villas, some of which have been excavated, dotted the fertile slopes of the mountain. Paintings of food, written accounts and remains of food found in Pompeii and Herculaneum indicate what was grown: vines, olives, wheat, barley, chickpeas, beans and cabbage. Herbs, onions, other vegetables and fruit were grown in smaller gardens and orchards, and honey was made to sweeten the wine. Pompeii was famous for its wine, which was exported to Rome and sold in the more than 130 bars and taverns in Pompeii itself. In one farm a wine press and wine cellars were found with amphorae (large jars) to store wine and olive oil. Olive oil was used for cooking, lighting and bathing (there was no soap as we know it).

Written sources indicate that sheep and pigs were reared. We know that one man in particular, called Numistrius, had dogs to guard his sheep and pigs. Paintings of eggs and the unfinished lunch of eggs left by temple priests at the time of the eruption show that chickens, too, were reared.

A number of bakeries have been found at Pompeii. Grain was ground between large millstones, turned by slaves using a wooden handle or by a donkey or horse. Bread, shaped into round loaves and divided into eight portions, was baked in large ovens. Eighty-one loaves of bread were still in one oven. A wall painting of a bakery shows the baker selling his bread, the round loaves stacked on top of his counter. Cakes were also made, and many cake moulds have been found.

A type of fish sauce called 'garum', made of dried fish and salt, seems to have been popular with Pompeians. The 'garum' factory must have smelt as Seneca, a Roman philosopher, complained about it.

△ Many bakeries have been found at Pompeii. The bread was baked in stone and brick ovens which used wood and shavings for fuel.

◁ This painted wall panel from Pompeii's neighbouring town of Herculaneum provides evidence of the wide range of food available around Vesuvius.

▽ The remains of the two-storey colonnade which surrounded three sides of the Forum, the town centre of Pompeii.

Cloth-making

Cloth-making was an important industry in Pompeii. Some houses had been converted into cloth factories. Wall paintings in these houses show the processes of washing, stretching, dying and drying cloth. From these we know that the raw cloth was cleaned by workers, often children, trampling it in large buckets full of a foul-smelling liquid concoction. It was rinsed, beaten, combed and then dried on lines or hung over a rounded wooden frame. Later it was placed in a wooden press to iron out the creases. Remains of presses have been found at Pompeii and Herculaneum. The raw wool probably came from the sheep in the countryside around the town.

The Forum

Like all Roman towns, Pompeii had a Forum, the town centre where the main government offices, banks, law courts, temples and market were located. Today we see the remains of the colonnade which surrounded three sides of the Forum square. Traders set up their stalls under the colonnade while offices were on the first floor. The walls are covered with painted advertisements, public notices and voting propaganda. Statues of gods, Roman emperors and important citizens of Pompeii are found throughout the Forum.

There are many temples in Pompeii. Some are dedicated to gods such as Venus, Jupiter and Apollo; others are dedicated to Roman emperors. A temple dedicated to the Egyptian goddess Isis is interesting because it shows that Egyptians also lived in Pompeii. Small shrines have been found on streets throughout the town and in most houses.

Leisure activities

The Pompeians seem to have enjoyed their leisure time. We know from the many bars and taverns that they drank wine with their friends, and a wall painting shows that they also played dice. In the early summer there must have been heated discussions about candidates standing for the local elections held each July. The political slogans and advertisements on walls surely caused much comment over a glass of wine.

It seems that sports were also well liked. The large Palaestra near the gladiators' barracks was a place to train, to take part in sports such as discus, long jump, wrestling, running and boxing, or just to walk around and watch others. A mosaic of fighting cocks suggests this game was also a favourite.

BATHING

Bathing was an important way of relaxing for the Romans. Some larger houses in Pompeii had private baths, but most people would have frequented the three main public baths – the Forum baths, the Stabian baths and the Central baths – located in the busiest parts of Pompeii. They had changing rooms, reading rooms, massage rooms, rest rooms, lecture rooms. These rooms were pleasant places, often brightly decorated. The Stabian baths also had a sports area, called the Palaestra, and a swimming pool. Women's baths were separated from men's.

These typical Roman baths had a hot bath (the caldarium), a warm steam-room (the tepidarium) and a cold bath (the frigidarium). Heat from a furnace flowed through channels under a thick concrete floor; this system is known as a hypocaust. Because the floors became very hot people wore thick-soled sandals to protect their feet.

Bathers were massaged with ointments which could be scraped off using a special instrument called a strigil. Strigils and ointment jars have been found during excavations. Over 1300 lamps were excavated at the Forum baths, which shows that they opened at night as well as during the day.

△ The caldarium (the hot bath) at the Forum Baths, with a wash basin at one end.

Gladiatorial combats

The most popular events took place in the oval amphitheatre. Twenty-five rows of seats could hold 20,000 people. The most important people sat in the lower or front seats and everyone else sat behind them. Shows included gladiatorial combats and fights between wild and tame animals. These events were advertised on the theatre walls, where the results were later posted. Sometimes fights broke out among the spectators.

One painting shows a fight in AD 59 between the Pompeians and their neighbours from Nocera when many people were killed. The event was recorded by Tacitus, who tells us that the amphitheatre was then closed on the order of the Emperor Nero. Ten years later his wife, the Empress Sabina Poppaea, a native of Pompeii, urged her husband to allow gladiatorial games to start again. The Pompeians wrote their appreciation on the walls: 'Three cheers for the decisions of the emperor and empress. Long live the Empress Poppaea.'

The gladiators' barracks were close to the amphitheatre. Excavations revealed all types of gladiatorial armour: helmets, shoulder guards, greaves (shin protectors) and ankle guards. Gladiators often enjoyed great popularity, as we see from the graffiti: 'Celadus, glory of the girls, heart-throb of the girls.'

The theatre

Two smaller theatres at Pompeii presented mimes, plays, clowning, dancing, juggling and musical events. Both theatres were horseshoe-shaped with rows of stone seats, enough to seat 5000 people in the larger theatre and 1200 in the smaller one, the Odeon. Sockets in the outside walls of the larger theatre held wooden poles for awnings, which sheltered the spectators from the hot sun.

The many wall paintings, mosaics and graffiti about the theatre show how much the Pompeians enjoyed it. Mosaics show actors wearing masks and preparing to go on stage, and street musicians with cymbals, drums, pipes and rattles. Musical instruments, too, have been found. As happens today, some actors

were greatly admired. Fans adorned the walls with their praises: 'Actius, darling of the people, come back quickly.'

Pompeii today

While the volcanic eruption of AD 79 covered and so preserved Pompeii for us, the excavations which have revealed it once more have brought their own problems. Years of exposure to wind, rain, sun and tourists are causing its destruction. The walls and wall paintings are gradually decaying. Grass and weeds grow through, and enlarge, cracks in mosaics. Millions of visitors wear down the streets. Some tourists even steal mementoes of the town, and in November 1980 another earthquake caused further damage. Restoration and conservation are therefore a vital part of work at Pompeii today.

△ A mosaic of actors choosing masks and preparing for a play. Mosaics are an important source of information about life at Pompeii. Unfortunately years of exposure to weather and throngs of visitors are causing mosaics, walls and wall paintings to deteriorate.

Photogrammetry, a technique for taking photographs from the air, has been used to make a plan of the town on which wall paintings and mosaics have been placed in their exact position. This and other data have been computerized so that information may be retrieved at the touch of a button.

Today, many such sophisticated techniques are used to preserve and protect Pompeii. Let us hope that generations to come may be able to search out and enjoy its secrets as so many have done in generations past.

THE VIKINGS IN NORTH AMERICA

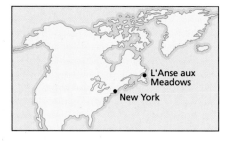

The search for ancient sites often requires a good deal of detective work inside a library, outside on the landscape, or both. Myths or legends can sometimes be used to help find archaeological sites. The discovery of a Viking settlement in Newfoundland, Canada, is an excellent example of the use of such documentary sources to locate an ancient site.

Unlike the Viking settlement in Canada, archaeological sites such as the Egyptian pyramids or Stonehenge have been known since the time of their construction. Archaeologists did not have to 'discover' them, although excavations were necessary to understand some of their secrets.

The Viking explorers

Most people regard the Vikings as brutal plunderers who raided the coasts of Europe. This is part of the truth. But the Vikings were also traders, farmers and hunters. They were adventurous and courageous explorers who colonized the most northerly and seemingly inhospitable lands of Iceland and Greenland. They even ventured as far as North America.

The Viking search for new regions was motivated by the need for farming land, especially good grazing land, which had become scarce in their homelands in Scandinavia. In the 9th century AD the

Vikings headed westward, occupying the Faeroe Islands and, later, Iceland. However, most of Iceland is uninhabitable, so the search for good land led them to venture even further west. In the 10th century, they settled in Greenland. In their continual quest for land, they explored the coasts of Greenland and parts of eastern North America.

Life in these northern lands was harsh and the winters were bitterly cold. But the grazing was good (although in restricted areas) and the fishing was excellent. The prospect of hunting was an added bonus. The Greenlanders sold furs and walrus ivory to European markets in exchange for European goods that were not available in Greenland.

INFORMATION FROM THE SAGAS

Tales were told about these Viking explorations; these were eventually written down and are called sagas. Some of the sagas describe the sea voyages of

▷ Page from the Greenlander Saga about Leif Ericsson's adventures in Vinland. It mentions Leif's departure from Vinland in the spring, his boat loaded with timber and grapes destined for Greenland.

▽ An artist's view of Viking life at L'Anse aux Meadows, part of the land referred to as Vinland in Viking sagas. The settlement may have been a base camp for boat repair, exploration and shipment of goods back to Greenland.

Eric the Red and Bjarni Herjolfsson, and the colonies founded by Leif Ericsson and Thorfinn Karlsefni in a land known as Vinland or Wineland. The sagas are an important source of information about Viking settlement in North America.

Eric the Red

The sagas begin with Eric the Red, a Norwegian. Exiled from Norway as a young man, he moved to Iceland. From there, in 982, he was once more banished, this time for three years. He decided to sail westward in search of a new land sighted 50 years previously but not explored. Eric's voyage of discovery was successful. He named the new land Greenland because he felt such a name would entice people to move there. Although most of it was inhospitable, there was some good land, very similar to that of his native Norway. A constant food supply was assured by the

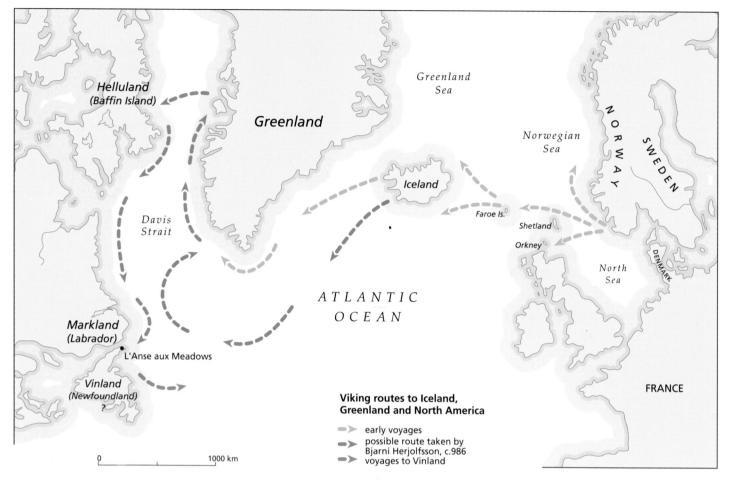

**Viking routes to Iceland,
Greenland and North America**

→ early voyages
→ possible route taken by
Bjarni Herjolfsson, c.986
→ voyages to Vinland

0 ——————— 1000 km

△ Intrepid seafarers, the Vikings regularly sailed between Scandinavia, Iceland and Greenland. Bjarni Herjolfsson discovered Vinland when his boat was blown off course on a voyage to Greenland.

abundance of animals and fish on the island and in the surrounding waters.

When his exile ended, Eric returned to Iceland. He organized a second expedition consisting of men, women and animals. The group set out to colonize Greenland. In their new land they built houses of turf and stones. The men hunted and fished while the women looked after the animals and houses. Viking settlement on Greenland lasted for 500 years.

Bjarni Herjolfsson's voyage

The Viking sagas continue with the story of Bjarni Herjolfsson, who left Iceland in 986 to visit his father in Greenland. He had no charts or compasses to guide him, only the descriptions of previous sailors.

It was, as always, a dangerous journey, and the ship got lost in dense fog. When the fog cleared, he saw land that

was forested and fairly flat. But there were no mountains, fjords or meadows, so Bjarni knew it was not Greenland. As he was anxious to see his father, he did not stop to explore, but changed direction and sailed northwards. For days the ship passed different regions, some flat and forested, others with mountains and glaciers, but none fitting the descriptions of Greenland. Once more Bjarni changed direction and finally he reached Greenland.

Leif Ericsson's voyage

The community in Greenland must have listened with excitement to Bjarni's accounts of the lands he had sighted, but they were too busy to think of exploring these unknown regions. Fifteen years later Leif Ericsson, Eric the Red's eldest son, set out to find them. The sagas tell of how Leif followed Bjarni's course, but in the opposite direction. He went ashore in three places. The first was a barren, grassless land of mountains and glaciers which he called Helluland (flatstone

land). Modern scholars believe this was part of what is now Baffin Island, off mainland Canada. The second place was wooded with low hills and long sandy beaches; he called this Markland (land of woods). It is thought to be along Canada's Labrador coast. Leif's third stop was in Vinland or Wineland.

There has been much controversy over the location of this legendary region. Many people now believe that northern Newfoundland, a Canadian province, may have been on the periphery of Vinland, or even formed part of it.

Settlement on Vinland

Leif and his crew first built a temporary camp. When they decided to stay for the winter they built long turf houses. The sagas mention that one of Leif's crew found grapes, which prompted Leif to name the land Vinland. This has been one of the major problems in the recent search for Vinland, as vines cannot grow in Newfoundland. We shall return to this important fact later.

The following spring Leif returned to Greenland full of enthusiasm about Vinland. He intended to return there. Sadly it was not to be: Leif's father Eric died and Leif then became leader of the Greenland colony. Over the next few years, however, his brothers and sister went to Vinland.

Thorvald Ericsson led the second voyage, and his party stayed in the houses Leif had built. The sagas tell how one day, while exploring the coastline, Thorvald's men met and killed some Native American people (or Skraelings as the Vikings called them). Later that night other Skraelings attacked the Vikings and Thorvald was killed by an arrow. As they were outnumbered by the Skraelings, Thorvald's men returned to Greenland the following spring.

This encounter with the Skraelings did not deter the Vikings. In 1008 Thorfinn Karlsefni sailed to Vinland with 160 men and women and some cattle and sheep. They settled there happily and began trading red cloth for furs and skins with the Skraelings. Unfortunately, relations with the Skraelings deteriorated and after three years the Viking settlers returned to Greenland.

Final contacts with Vinland

A further voyage to Vinland was led by Eric's daughter Freydis. Her group stayed for one year, collecting timber to sell in Greenland. There were fewer voyages to Vinland after the year 1020, although the Vikings continued to live in Greenland.

Viking artefacts have been found on many Inuit sites both in Arctic Canada and in Greenland, indicating that the two groups must have traded with each other quite peacefully throughout the remaining 450 years of Viking occupation of Greenland.

THE SEARCH FOR VINLAND

Viking sites are well known in Iceland and Greenland, but Vinland proved elusive. Where was it? The sagas mention that grapes and wheat grew in Vinland. This suggests a region where the climate allows them to grow. For 100 years people searched for Vinland, claiming to find it in New England, Rhode Island, Maine and Minnesota in the United States of America, and in Nova Scotia in Canada. But all these claims were false.

A modern Viking explorer

In the 1950s a modern Viking, Dr Helge Ingstad, entered the story. He was a Norwegian explorer. He carefully studied the Viking settlements in Greenland, read the Viking sagas and examined maps. He concluded that Vinland began in northern Newfoundland. Saga descriptions of the journey from Greenland to Vinland and the travelling times mentioned supported Ingstad's theory. However, knowing that vines do not grow in Newfoundland, he first searched the coast further south between Rhode Island and Nova Scotia. He found no trace of Viking settlement.

In 1960 Ingstad conducted an aerial survey of the Newfoundland and Labrador coast looking for areas similar to the saga descriptions. The survey continued by boat in those areas which looked promising. He stopped at fishing villages and inspected many sites.

▽ L'Anse aux Meadows, location of the only Viking settlement in North America discovered so far. Its exposed position made it unsuitable for long-term colonization, but it could be easily spotted by Viking sailors arriving from Greenland.

He asked villagers if there were any unusual mounds or old house sites in the region, but without success.

Then one day he arrived at a small fishing village called L'Anse aux Meadows. It was in a region of forests, low undulating hills, small lakes and large expanses of meadow. The area fitted the saga accounts. A fisherman, George Decker, took Ingstad to the nearby Épaves Bay. He pointed to outlines of old house sites and mounds by a small river. It seemed to Ingstad that this was just the type of landscape the Vikings liked to settle, with its rich fields for grazing, fresh water and nearby sea. He thought of Viking settlements in similar locations in Greenland. Only archaeological excavations would reveal if it was a Viking site.

The excavations

Ingstad's wife, the archaeologist Anne Stine Ingstad, led the excavations. Three house sites were visible as depressions in the ground. The first excavations took place in the summer of 1961. A series of test trenches was cut to get an idea of what lay beneath the surface. This showed the houses to be simple structures with open hearths and cooking pits. But no tools or implements were found to indicate who had built them.

After some weeks the excavation team left L'Anse aux Meadows to investigate the coast further north. At the end of August Anne Stine Ingstad returned to the site to continue excavating with a group of villagers. One evening, when the sun was low in the sky (a good time to see features on the ground), she noticed an uneven patch of ground. Test trenches revealed a house which was similar to Viking houses. The team also found old, corroded iron rivets (a type of nail) and hearths similar to those found in Viking settlements in Iceland and Greenland.

Anne Stine Ingstad was sure she had found a Viking house; indeed, she believed she might have found part of Vinland. She decided to extend the excavations the following year.

△ A shallow depression in the ground is all that remains of one of the Viking houses at L'Anse aux Meadows. Archaeologists discovered eight buildings which formed three distinct groups. The houses consisted of a large multi-roomed hall, a living room, a workshop and a storage area. A furnace workshop was located slightly away from the dwellings.

A Viking site

Seven summer seasons of excavation by the Ingstad team and four by a team from the Canadian Parks Service indicate that L'Anse aux Meadows is indeed a Viking site. Eight buildings were revealed. These formed three groups, each with a large dwelling house, a workshop and a storage area. The buildings were made of turf, the same material as the Vikings used for houses in Iceland and Greenland. Peat bogs around the site would have provided an ample supply of building material.

The most recent carbon 14 dates (see pages 26–27) indicate that the site was occupied sometime between 980 and 1020. Archaeologists also studied the architecture of houses on other Viking sites built in different periods. They compared these houses with the houses at L'Anse aux Meadows and deduced that the site must have been occupied early in the 11th century. Both the carbon 14 dates and the architectural data are consistent with the dates given in the sagas, and indicate that the Vinland voyages must have taken place between 1000 and 1020.

Where is Vinland?

The houses, artefacts, dates and description of the area all agree with the saga descriptions. But what about the grapes? Vines cannot grow in Newfoundland. Yet the sagas speak of grapes. Some researchers claim that the sagas were rewritten and changed over the centuries, and that the earliest ones do not in fact mention grapes. Other specialists suggest that settlers brought grapes to the settlement from voyages further south along the eastern coast of North America.

Dr Helge Ingstad proposes another alternative. He maintains that the word 'vin' in Vinland means meadow and suggests that Leif Ericsson named the area after its rich meadows. However, most scholars disagree with Helge's suggestion.

Recently, Birgitta Wallace, director of the later excavations at L'Anse aux Meadows, has suggested that the site was a Viking base camp where boats were repaired. It was located at the entrance to Vinland, which extended further inland. She notes that three butternuts (a type of walnut) were found on the site, which could have been brought there only by humans. The closest area where butternut trees grow is in New Brunswick, south of L'Anse aux Meadows. Wild grapes could flourish in this area too. She suggests that the Vikings called the entire region they explored Vinland, although grapes grew in just one area. Viking Vinland, says Birgitta Wallace, may be the southern part of the Gulf of St Lawrence. If this is so, then surely more Viking sites await discovery.

▽ Reconstruction of one of the Viking houses at L'Anse aux Meadows. The houses were made of timber and covered with turf (earth and grass). Only the lower levels of turf were preserved and revealed in excavation, but impressions of the collapsed turf roof were found along the inner walls.

VIKING HOUSES AND ARTEFACTS

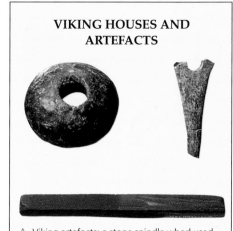

△ Viking artefacts: a stone spindle whorl used to spin wool, a bone needle and a needle hone – a needle-sharpening stone.

Large and small hearths filled with ashes and charcoal were found in the houses at L'Anse aux Meadows. Most houses had stone-lined ember pits, where glowing embers were placed at night and covered with ashes to keep them burning. In the morning the fire could then be rekindled quickly. Similar ember pits have been found in Viking settlements in Iceland and Greenland. The earthen floors had been hardened and blackened with specks of charcoal. Earthen sleeping platforms had been built along the walls. Small round depressions in the floors were probably holes for the timber posts which would have supported the roofs.

Distinctive Viking artefacts were found in and near the house sites. These include a number of iron nails, rivets, and fragments of slag iron, the waste remaining from smelting iron. The Native American people and Inuits of that time did not know how to make metal, but the Vikings did. The archaeologists were sure that the Vikings made their own iron at the site, but where did the iron ore (from which iron is made) come from? They began to investigate the areas near the settlement and soon found the source in nearby bogs. Later, they found a blacksmith's workshop, with an iron smelting furnace; a little further away was a charcoal kiln. There were so many small pieces of iron that the archaeologists used magnets to collect them.

TENOCHTITLÁN: GREAT CITY OF THE AZTECS

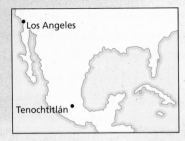

The first cities in the world developed in Europe, North Africa and Asia between 3000 BC and 2000 BC. These were the cities of the Sumerians of Mesopotamia (mainly present-day Iraq), the Egyptians, and the Indus peoples of Pakistan and India. The first cities in Mesoamerica arose a little later, about 1200 BC, and are associated with a culture we call the Olmecs.

The last of the great native Meso-american cities was the Aztec city of Tenochtitlán in the Valley of Mexico. It was the capital of the largest empire in Mesoamerica at the time of the Spanish conquest in 1521. It was also larger and better organized than any European city of the 16th century.

Mexico and Central America formed part of an ancient region archaeologists call Mesoamerica. For thousands of years it was home to groups of nomads, some of whom later settled and began to farm. Settlements grew, with true cities emerging about 1200 BC. Tenochtitlán was founded much later in the 14th century AD.

The fall of Tenochtitlán

On 13 August 1521, after a 70-day siege, the explorer Hernán Cortés claimed the city of Tenochtitlán for the King of Spain. The splendour of the city amazed the triumphant Spaniards. Their historians described it as 'like the things of enchantment… because of the great towers and temples and buildings that rose up out of the water, and all made of stone mason-ry… never was there seen, nor heard, nor even dreamt, anything like that which we then observed.' The fall of Tenochtitlán to the Spanish in that fateful year proved to be the death knell for the Aztec Empire.

▷ The present-day Mexico City lies above Tenochtitlán. Parts of the great Aztec city have been revealed as a result of construction work over the past 200 years, particularly during the building of the underground railway in the 1960s. The temple of Ehecatl-Quetzalcoatl was found in 1967 when the Pino Suarez metro station was built.

◁ An artist's impression of what the main temple precinct of Tenochtitlán may have looked like. The 16th-century Spanish conquerors demolished the Aztec capital and built their own city on the ruins. Reconstruction of the city centre is based on archaeological and documentary evidence. Surrounded by a wall, the sacred area was dominated by a large pyramid on top of which were the twin temples to Tlaloc, the rain god, and Huitzilopochtli, god of sun and war.

CODICES

▷ Codices were long, folded strips of paper on which the Aztecs illustrated and wrote about their life and history.

▽ Discipline and work of Aztec children. Naughty 11-year-olds had to breathe in acrid smoke, a boy of 12 had to lie on the damp ground with hands and feet tied, and a girl was woken and made to sweep the house. Children of 11 and 12 received one and a half tortillas (corn bread) a day. Boys of 13 and 14 collected reeds and fished; girls learnt to grind corn and weave. They received two tortillas a day.

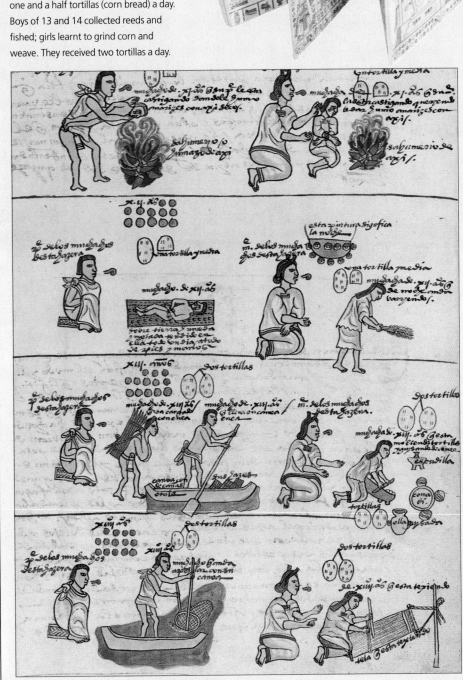

The Aztecs themselves wrote about their way of life in books called codices. These were pictorial descriptions of Aztec life and history. They consisted of long strips of paper, made of birch bark and folded rather like a large fan, quite unlike the type of book with which we are familiar. Most codices were destroyed by the Spaniards after the conquest, but luckily for us some have survived.

Much of the information we have about the Aztecs comes from the writings of the Spanish missionaries, who were sent to Mexico soon after the conquest to convert the local populations to Christianity. They learnt the Aztec language in order to find out about the Aztecs' beliefs and their way of life.

One such missionary, Friar Bernardino de Sahagún, arrived in Mexico in 1529. He discovered that the Aztecs had hidden some codices. His Aztec helpers showed him these codices and explained each picture to him. During the following 30 years Sahagún compiled a 12-volume history of Aztec life. Some of Cortés' own soldiers also wrote about the sights they saw – sights which were both wondrous and gruesome. These Spanish writings are often called chronicles.

In addition, archaeology has provided us with information on all aspects of Aztec life. The combination of information from written and archaeological sources has given us a fairly complete picture of Aztec life, customs and beliefs.

Today, the remains of Tenochtitlán for the most part lie hidden from sight below Mexico City, the city founded by the 16th-century Spanish conquerors. Although most of Tenochtitlán is lost to us, we know much about the Aztecs and their capital from both historical and archaeological sources.

Uncovering the lost city

But how do you find the remains of an ancient civilization which lie beneath a large modern city like Mexico City? You cannot dig holes underneath large buildings; they could collapse. As with all large cities where generations have lived for hundreds, even thousands, of years, discovering the physical remains of the past is a question of luck. Indeed, such has been the case with the Aztec capital and Mexico City.

Tantalizing evidence of the past has been uncovered during construction work over the last 200 years: carved sculptures, parts of stone stairways, fragments of wall paintings. 20th-century archaeologists have used the occasions when buildings are demolished to undertake small excavations on the sites before new buildings are erected.

Discovery of the Great Temple

Luck was on the archaeologists' side when the Mexican government decided to build an underground railway system in Mexico City. During construction, which began in 1966, a wealth of Aztec artefacts was unearthed. And then, on 21 February 1978, electricity workers digging in the centre of Mexico City uncovered part of a huge carved stone. Work ceased immediately and archaeologists were contacted.

After four days of careful excavation, a massive stone carving of the Aztec moon goddess was revealed. The archaeologists knew they had uncovered part of the Great Temple of the Aztecs, the most sacred place in the Aztec world and the centre of Tenochtitlán, the Aztec capital. This was truly a discovery of great importance. The Mexican authorities decided that further excavation of the area was essential and asked Professor Matos Moctezuma, an experienced Mexican archaeologist, to direct the excavations.

△ The accidental exposure of the huge stone goddess Coyolxauhqui by electricity workers in 1978 led to the discovery of the Great Temple of the Aztecs.

Preparing for the excavation

Before undertaking any excavation archaeologists must make careful plans. They must decide what they want to do and know why they want to do it, what questions they hope to answer, and what techniques they are going to use. They must also have as much background knowledge as possible. Moctezuma and his team of specialists carefully read the 16th-century Spanish chronicles describing Tenochtitlán and Aztec life to get an idea of what the Great Temple looked like. This would help them recognize objects and parts of the temple as they excavated them; it would also help them understand what they meant to the Aztecs themselves. It was an important aspect of preparing for the excavation.

Equally crucial was working out how to excavate a large area in the centre of a busy modern city without destroying the surrounding buildings. Although these buildings were from periods after the Aztecs, many were also of historical importance. In the end, only two buildings were demolished, but not before those sections of particular historical significance had been photographed extensively.

The excavators also had to take into account the underground water table, which was not far beneath the city. As Tenochtitlán had been built on an island, the archaeologists could not excavate the lowest levels of the site as this might have caused the temple and parts of the modern city to collapse. When preparations were complete, Moctezuma and his team began their excavations. These lasted for four years from 1978 to 1982.

WHAT WE KNOW ABOUT TENOCHTITLÁN

The 16th-century Spanish chronicles tell us that in AD 1325 the Aztecs founded Tenochtitlán on an island surrounded by a swampy lake in the Valley of Mexico. Within less than a hundred years, Tenochtitlán had grown into a huge city of 150,000 to 200,000 inhabitants. It was connected to the mainland by three wide roads, one to the north, one to the south and one to the west. Travel within the city was often along waterways, much like modern Venice. In the centre of the city was an immense ceremonial centre with many temples and shrines, dominated by the Great Temple.

The Great Temple was built in the form of a pyramid, the front of which faced towards the west. A double stairway led to two smaller temples at the summit. These were dedicated to the most important of the Aztec gods: Huitzilopochtli, the god of sun and war, and Tlaloc, the god of rain and water. Numerous stone statues, figurines and masks of Tlaloc have been found in the excavation, but none of Huitzilopochtli. We know from the Spanish chronicles that his image was usually made with a special type of dough and seeds. Such images therefore would have disintegrated long ago.

Tribute paid to the ruler

At the time of the Spanish conquest, the Aztec empire extended over most of Mexico. Every town conquered by the Aztecs had to pay tribute (a type of tax) to the ruler in Tenochtitlán. Aztec codices record vast amounts of food being received from the provinces – maize (corn), beans, fruit, cacao, honey and chillis.

Tribute also included cotton, wood, military uniforms, headdresses, shields, clothes, paper, pottery, reed mats, precious stones, jewellery, turquoise and stone masks, featherwork, gold, silver, animal skins, sea shells and slaves.

The payment of such tribute caused great hardship to the conquered towns, and we read of rebellions which were cruelly punished by Aztec armies. Indeed, many of these tribute-paying peoples were only too delighted to welcome the Spanish invaders and to help them destroy the detested Aztecs.

The workers of Tenochtitlán also paid a form of tribute to their ruler. They had to give him some of their produce; this might have been what they grew in their fields, the fish they caught or what they made with their hands. They also worked for him on public projects such as building temples, and when needed they fought for him as soldiers.

Farming

Agriculture was very important in Tenochtitlán. Aztec codices and Spanish chronicles tell us that Aztec farmers created artificial strips of land using mud and weeds from the swamp in which they lived.

These artificially raised fields, called chinampas, were separated by canals. The sides of the chinampas were protected by wooden stakes, and trees planted along the edges prevented the earth from sliding back into the swamp.

The Aztec chinampas were amazingly fertile. Farmers grew a wide range of crops including maize, chilli, tomatoes, squash, beans, herbs and flowers, which they took to the huge market in the Tlatelolco district of Tenochtitlán.

△ Mexico City is one of the largest cities in the world. Lake Texcoco, on which the city is built, has almost disappeared.

◁ A 16th-century map of Tenochtitlán. The city was built on a lake and linked to the mainland by causeways.

▷ The gardens of Xochimilco in southern Mexico City are all that remain of the fertile Aztec chinampa fields.

△ Painting of Tenochtitlán market by Diego Rivera. Food, gold, feathers, jewellery, pottery, animal skins, flint and obsidian knives and a host of other objects were sold there.

The Tenochtitlán market

The descriptions of Tenochtitlán market by Spanish soldiers show that they had never before seen such a huge and efficiently run market where so many different products were bought and sold. Special areas were set aside for each type of produce and everything was carefully controlled. Those who stole or cheated were severely punished. There was no money as we know it; people exchanged their goods or paid with cacao beans, copper axes or lengths of cloth.

Living areas

Spanish writers tell us of the splendid houses and palaces of the Aztec ruler and his nobles. Some were huge, often with gardens on an upper level as well as at ground level. Orchards, herb gardens, and pools stocked with exotic fish were common in the gardens of the nobility. The ruler's palace was a place of wonder. It had an armoury, a textile room where women wove cloth for the ruler and workshops for potters, metal workers, jewellers and a host of other skilled workers. There was also an aviary with all kinds of birds from distant parts of the empire. Those who saw the palace gardens describe them as a place of wonder and magnificence.

▷ The Great Temple of Tenochtitlán was rebuilt at least six times. The Aztecs did not destroy earlier temples: they preserved them by building on top of and around them.

The Aztec ruler and his nobles lived in the centre of Tenochtitlán, close to the ceremonial area. The rest of the population lived further away from the Great Temple. They lived in groups called calpulli, consisting of their relatives or those who did the same type of work. Each clan or calpulli lived in their own neighbourhood, in small one-storey houses. These were made of wattle and daub – a mixture of mud and twigs – or adobe, the American term for sun-dried mudbricks.

Enter archaeology

Eyewitness accounts provide a detailed picture of Aztec life at Tenochtitlán. Archaeological excavation has done much to bring these written accounts to life. The excavations directed by Professor Matos Moctezuma covered between 5000 and 7000 square metres of the centre of Mexico City.

Excavation revealed a giant pyramid structure which had been rebuilt at least six times. The topmost level was demolished by the Spanish conquerors, who used the stone to build their own city. Luckily much more remains of the lower levels which the Spanish did not see. The lowest part was not uncovered during excavation because of the high water table, but we know from historical sources that this was the first temple built by the

Aztecs when they founded Tenochtitlán in AD 1325. The intervening levels have provided us with a great deal of information to add to our knowledge of the Aztecs, much of which we can verify through the historical sources.

Excavation of the Great Temple

As each new temple was added, the previous one was covered over and the next temple built on top of it. At the top of the second temple, the lowest level uncovered during the excavation, the excavators found shrines similar to those dedicated to the gods Huitzilopochtli and Tlaloc.

A stone, where human sacrifices were made, was found in front of the shrine to Huitzilopochtli. The size of the stone and the practice of human sacrifice are both reported by the 16th-century chroniclers. A large statue, called a chacmool, was found in front of the Tlaloc shrine, and more statues were found inside the painted shrines.

Aztec writing, known as glyphs, was found on part of the staircase; this provides a date which, according to the Aztec calendar, corresponds to 1390, the date when this particular temple was built. Glyphs at other levels have allowed the archaeologists to date the construction of some of the other temples.

Stone sculptures, carvings on stone and offerings of artefacts were found in all of the excavated temples. In the third temple (dated to 1431), for example, eight life-size statues were found at the bottom of the staircase. In the fourth temple (1454), the excavations uncovered stone braziers (probably used for burning incense); these were decorated with symbols of the gods Huitzilopochtli and Tlaloc. Serpent heads adorned the sides of the temple.

Archaeologists have used many different forms of information to help unravel the secrets of Tenochtitlán that are hidden underground. Professor Matos Moctezuma has successfully used the writings of the 16th-century Spanish chroniclers, the codices of the Aztecs themselves and archaeological excavation to provide us with a detailed understanding of Mexico's exotic past.

OFFERINGS TO THE GODS

▷ Double-headed serpents are often mentioned in Mesoamerican mythology. This one, made of wood covered by a turquoise mosaic, could have been worn on ritual occasions; it may have been among the treasure offered to Cortés by the Aztec ruler, Motecuhzoma II.

The Aztecs made many offerings to their gods. Those found inside the Great Temple are offerings in honour of Huitzilopochtli and Tlaloc. The offerings were found in three specific contexts: in small stone-walled rooms, inside stone boxes, and in holes in the earth covering an earlier temple. Most offerings were near the front of the Great Temple or near the shrines to the gods. The artefacts were always placed very carefully, often in special positions facing in a particular direction. We know, then, that the position of these objects had a special meaning for the Aztecs.

More than 6000 artefacts were excavated from offering contexts. Many came from distant parts of the empire, particularly the coastal regions. Among these were shells, corals and a variety of fish. Turtle and crocodile remains were also found, but only parts of these reptiles were used, usually the turtle shell and only the skin and head of crocodiles. Similarly the skull and skin of snakes were buried, but not the whole body.

Spanish writers mention Aztec offerings but do not speak of marine objects, which were often found among the excavated offerings. They comment on the common custom of making bird offerings, but few of these were found in the excavations. Professor Matos Moctezuma suggests that birds were the usual everyday offerings, while marine animals were used for special occasions such as those celebrated in the Great Temple. Animal offerings, in particular, had a special meaning, and were carefully placed in a special order. One of the most spectacular is the skeleton of a jaguar with a greenstone ball in its mouth.

Many offerings found in the Great Temple represent the Aztec gods Huitzilopochtli or Tlaloc. Although no statues or masks of Huitzilopochtli have been found in the excavation, objects such as skulls, knives and artefacts from conquered areas are fitting symbols for the god of war.

UNDERWATER ARCHAEOLOGY

Today underwater excavation is a flourishing branch of archaeology. The development of sophisticated diving equipment during the last 50 years has allowed archaeologists to excavate many underwater sites. Among these are submerged lakeside settlements, ancient wells and springs, and marine sites such as sunken cities, harbours and shipwrecks.

Some of the very earliest underwater investigations occurred more than 100 years ago in Switzerland. Wooden house posts were exposed when the water level of Lake Geneva was unusually low. Excavations revealed the remains of a Neolithic lakeside settlement which had been drowned by the rising water level of the lake.

In the early 19th century English divers made a living by searching the murky waters around Portsmouth for shipwrecks. These early underwater explorations were accomplished using primitive diving bells, suits and helmets.

But why go under water when there are so many sites on land awaiting investigation? Excavation of land sites is expensive, but underwater excavation is a much more expensive and complex undertaking. However, the knowledge to be gained from underwater investigation justifies the time and expense. The study of shipwrecks shows us how shipbuilding developed from small prehistoric dugout canoes to the mighty warships of the 16th century and later. Excavations of shipwrecks have also greatly increased our knowledge of maritime trade routes during the Bronze Age over 3500 years ago, and in later Greek, Roman and medieval times. Organic materials such as leather, food, clothing and wood, often well preserved in underwater sites, provide information that is lacking on most land sites. As with all sudden natural disasters, shipwrecks provide a glimpse of life at a specific moment in time.

Discovering underwater sites

Sites are commonly located by fishermen whose nets get caught on underwater obstructions. Many Mediterranean sites have been found by divers searching for sponges. Others are revealed through the dredging of rivers and harbours. Survey techniques such as aerial survey and sophisticated methods of subsurface detection which are used on land can also be applied under water.

◁ A diver bringing an amphora (storage jar) to the surface near the coast of Turkey. Since ancient times people have used ships to transport goods. Sometimes ships sink – a disaster for traders but a delight for archaeologists.

ARCHAEOLOGICAL TECHNIQUES UNDER WATER

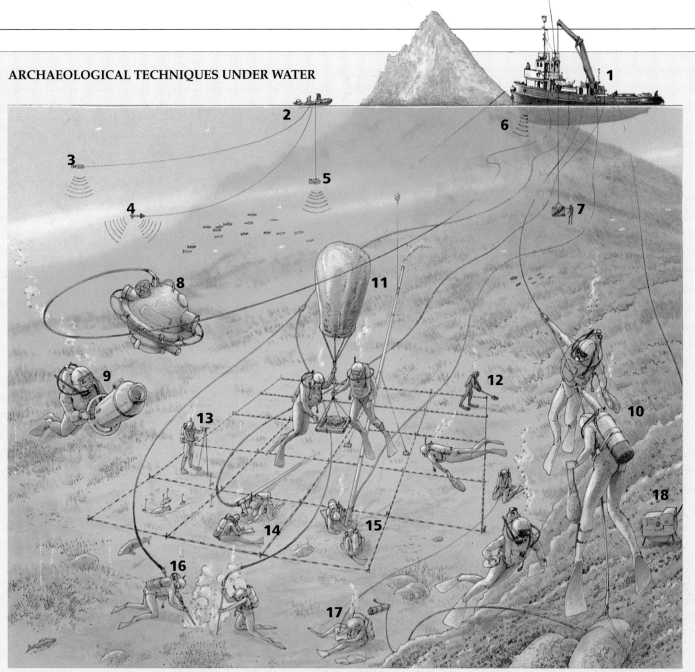

Poor visibility, the cold, tides and problems associated with depth can make underwater excavation difficult. Because of these problems expensive support ships, anchored above the site, may be needed. With the correct equipment divers can work under water for relatively long periods of time. They must, however, return to the surface gradually to allow their bodies to adjust to the changing levels of air pressure. They may also have to spend time in a recompression chamber on the diving support vessel.

Many excavation techniques used on land are adapted for use under water. Grids can be laid out to help in mapping and drawing the site and marking the location of objects, and to help the divers as they excavate. The grids have to be weighted down to prevent them from moving in the water. Recording, drawing, mapping and photography are done with instruments which can be used under water. Various techniques are used to lift objects and sediments: air bags are used to raise baskets of objects, while air pipes suck up debris and sediments. Heavy objects weigh less under water and sometimes the diver can bring them up to the ship. Post-excavation work begins on board the research ship and continues at a laboratory on land.

△ Techniques used in underwater excavation:

1–2 Diving vessels monitor the excavations and provide accommodation, storage, workspace, recompression chamber and communications.

3–6 Seabed scanning devices.

7 Winch for lifting heavy loads.

8 Remote-operated vehicle with video and cameras.

9 Diver using underwater scooter.

10 Divers returning to surface along a line.

11 Air balloon used to lift artefacts.

12 Metal detector to explore edge of site.

13 Surveying.

14–15 Excavating using a water dredge and airlift to remove silts.

16 Probing seabed with water lances.

17 Recording measurements.

18 TV camera relays images to surface ship.

THE *MARY ROSE*: HENRY VIII'S WARSHIP

The story of the English ship, the *Mary Rose*, demonstrates how a wide variety of archaeological techniques applied to a shipwreck have succeeded in providing us with a detailed history of a 16th-century warship and a vivid picture of life on board.

Some early accounts of the *Mary Rose* refer to the costs of transporting the new ship from the Thames in London to Portsmouth. They mention her success in earlier campaigns against the French and they make glowing references to her power. Her last moments are detailed in eyewitness accounts of how she sank during battle against the French fleet near Portsmouth harbour on 19 July 1545.

The *Mary Rose* sank with most of her crew of 415 or more, watched by horrified crowds on shore, among them Henry VIII. As the ship capsized water poured in through the gunports, which were open for action. The water and weight of goods

△ Artist's reconstruction of the *Mary Rose* as she was in 1545, based on evidence from the remains of the ship recovered during excavation.

on board caused the ship to sink so rapidly that she became entombed in the soft sediments of the seabed. About 35 men survived the disaster.

Early salvage attempts

Records detail payments made to individuals attempting (unsuccessfully) to salvage the ship in the years following the disaster. Between 1547 and 1549, for example, an Italian called Peter Paul was paid for guns he had recovered from the ship. However, after 1549 all salvage efforts were abandoned. Those parts of the ship exposed on the seabed were gradually broken by sea action and wood-boring creatures. The rest of the ship slowly disappeared beneath the seabed.

Occasionally strong currents moved the sediments and exposed timbers. In 1836

fishermen complained about obstructions on the seabed which were affecting their fishing lines. They contacted John and Charles Deane, divers who had invented a diving suit and helmet with a hose attached to it which allowed them to breathe under water. The Deanes, who lived by searching for lost wrecks, began their underwater investigations and discovered a wreck, the *Mary Rose*.

They recovered parts of 24 guns, as well as gun-carriages, longbows, pottery, cloth, and a number of human skulls. Although they did not draw plans locating their finds, the Deanes made detailed illustrations of them. By 1840 they decided no more could be salvaged from the ship and stopped work. Once again the *Mary Rose* was forgotten.

Modern search for the *Mary Rose*

In 1965 Alexander McKee, an amateur diver, undertook a project to look for wrecks in the Portsmouth area. He invited archaeologist Margaret Rule to join him. Using eyewitness accounts and an 1841 naval chart marking the spot where the Deanes had discovered the *Mary Rose*, McKee and his divers began their search. It was a long, arduous job but eventually, with the aid of sophisticated acoustic (sound) devices, they discovered the ship. In 1978 a trench excavated across the wreck showed that much of the ship was 'in situ' (in almost the same position as when it had sunk). It was decided to excavate the ship and its contents.

The *Mary Rose* was excavated between 1979 and 1982. During this time more than 16,000 finds were recovered from the seabed and recorded. On 11 October 1982, more than 400 years after she had sunk, the ship was finally raised and taken back to Portsmouth.

The ship's decks

Excavation revealed the remains of four decks above the hold of the ship, each with its own function. Ballast of broken fragments of black flint was kept in the hold to give the ship stability, along with stores of wood for the huge brick galley (kitchen). Four large cauldrons (three used for cooking and one to store pitch – for making

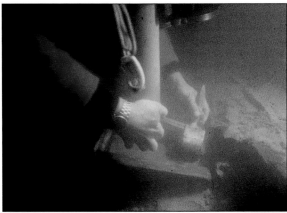

△ Silt, carefully removed during excavation in the murky Portsmouth waters, is carried away by a pump.

▷ Cushioned in a steel cradle, the *Mary Rose* is raised to the surface by a crane on 11 October 1982, 437 years after she had sunk.

the seams and joints of the ship watertight), frying pans and a pair of bellows were among the finds in the galley.

The Orlop deck, directly above the hold, was divided into small compartments, mostly used for storage. Spare axles, wheels, rigging, cables, coils of anchor cable, rope, boxes of bows and arrows, a barrel of candles and wooden lanterns were found on this deck. Wooden chests containing the personal possessions of seamen and officers were found in some compartments.

Guns still on their gun-carriages were located on the three upper decks. Some were at open gunports ready for action.

All guns (including those found by the Deanes) were loaded and ready to fire. The equipment to load and fire them lay nearby. During post-excavation work it was discovered that one of the Deanes' guns fitted on to a gun-carriage excavated in 1981. Along the top deck a series of movable screens or blinds was found.

▷ Remains of the *Mary Rose* in dry dock in Portsmouth. She had four decks above the hold. The hold and the Orlop deck, immediately above it, were used largely for storage and to hold ballast. The galley (kitchen) was in the hold. Guns and hand weapons were found on the Main and Upper decks, where the surgery and sailors' cabins were located. The top or Castle deck was equipped with guns. The ship itself was made mostly of oak wood. It has been estimated that trees from almost 36 acres of land would have been needed to build it.

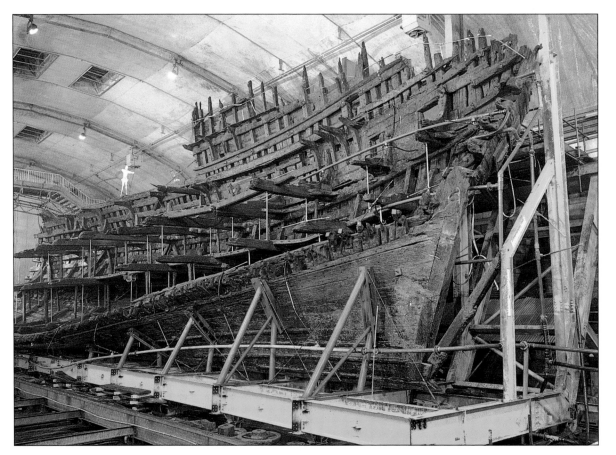

▽ Five ceramic jars, made in Germany and carefully sealed with corks, were found in the doctor's surgery. They had once contained medicines but we do not know what they were.

These could be dropped over the gun or archery stations to protect the seamen and removed when no longer needed.

The archers were preparing to fight when the ship sank; bows, arrows and other archery equipment were retrieved from the gun-decks. Most seamen on the *Mary Rose* would have been competent archers as they were obliged by law to practise archery from childhood.

Fragments of netting were found on the top deck, which had been covered with netting to deter enemy attackers from boarding the ship. As the ship sank it obstructed escape. Many skeletons were found trapped under the netting.

Life on the *Mary Rose*

The excavation provides us with a detailed picture of the fighting mechanisms of a 16th-century warship. It tells us about the seamen's life on board: their medicines, their food, their clothes and their leisure time. This kind of information is often lacking in archaeological excavations on land because it comes mainly from organic materials which have usually disintegrated and dissolved. Luckily many organic objects on the *Mary Rose* were buried beneath the seabed under fine silts in an anaerobic

(oxygen-free) environment. Consequently destructive bacteria could not grow and objects made from leather, silk, wool and wood were often recovered in a superb state of preservation.

The doctor's surgery

Two small compartments, located on the lowest gun-deck near the fighting, belonged to the ship's doctor, known at the time as the barber surgeon. A bench and wooden medicine chest were found in one compartment. The chest contained a jar of peppercorns, used to cure agues (fevers) and quinsy (inflammation of the throat), and nine jars of ointments, some partly used and some showing fingerprints from the last hand to touch them. Bandages ready for use, syringes and surgical tools were also stored in the chest. Other items in the barber surgeon's cabin included a mortar for grinding drugs, wooden jars, glass bottles, pewter canisters and plates, leather shoes, and a purse containing silver coins. The barber surgeon's velvet hat was found. A 16th-century painting of barber surgeons shows them wearing similar hats.

The sailors' diet

Pork, beef, mutton, venison and fish bones packed in barrels or baskets in the ship's stores show that the sailors ate well. Fishing lines were found in one seaman's chest, suggesting that some men added extra fish to their diet. Vegetables included fresh peas (still in their pod when

excavated). Fruit, too, was available, as plum or prune stones were recovered. Herbs and spices, including peppercorns, gave extra flavour to the food.

Eating and drinking utensils were also recovered: officers used pewter plates, tankards and spoons, while the lower ranks used wooden utensils.

The clothes they wore

During post-excavation work researchers made detailed drawings of the many fragments of wool, leather and silk clothing recovered. They made patterns of the garments and used them to reconstruct parts of clothing which were missing. Specialists worked out how the clothes were worn and estimated the size of the people who wore them. Shoes, a variety of leather jerkins, often laced at the sides or front, and fragments of knitted garments, including woollen stockings, have survived well. Ribbons, thread, buttons, pins and thimbles were found among the seamen's personal possessions. The men probably used them to darn and patch some of the clothes recovered from the excavation. Two leather caps are similar to those seen in contemporary paintings. No underclothes or breeches have been preserved. These were probably made from linen, most of which has almost entirely disappeared.

△ Many different types of leather shoes, some in a bag awaiting repair, were recovered during excavation of the *Mary Rose*.

Off-duty pastimes

When off duty the men entertained themselves with games, music and books. Games, including backgammon, dice and counters, were found in the crew's cabins and stored in the officers' personal seachests. Several types of wind instruments, fragments of fiddles, a drum and a small wooden whistle were recovered. Some of the pipes may have been used to pipe orders to the men, while others were undoubtedly played for pleasure. The finest instrument, a type of oboe called a shawm, was found with its case near the barber surgeon's cabin.

Although no books have survived, a number of leather book covers were recovered. These, along with quill pens and inkwells, show that some men, probably the officers, were able to read and write. Most of the crew, however, would have been illiterate. (Many objects have their owner's marks on them. Important areas of the ship are clearly marked with symbols. Some guns and gun parts were also marked to show that the different things were to be used together.)

Conserving the evidence

Once excavated from their protective, anaerobic home, all organic objects had to be treated to prevent the process of decay which begins as soon as they are exposed to air. Iron, bronze, lead, pewter and ceramic artefacts also needed to be cleaned and protected. Conservation of objects found in the *Mary Rose* began as soon as they were recovered. On board the research ship all objects were packed in airtight bags before removal to the onshore laboratory, where they were kept in airtight conditions until they could be properly conserved. There are so many objects that the programme of conservation has not yet finished.

The largest and longest job for conservators was the ship itself. Today the *Mary Rose* is in dry dock in Portsmouth, kept in a special environment and sprayed with a chemical wax to preserve it. Henry VIII's gallant warship is both a memorial to the men who lost their lives in the 16th century and a tribute to the 20th-century team of dedicated archaeological experts who recovered her.

△ Instruments found on board include three tabor pipes and part of a stringed instrument, probably a fiddle. The piper played the pipes with one hand while tapping a tabor (small drum) with the other.

◁ Many leather items have been recovered from the *Mary Rose* and have been carefully conserved. Here a specialist completes the reconstruction of a leather bucket.

DISCOVERING OUR INDUSTRIAL PAST

Remains of the industrial age – machines, engines, factories, warehouses, mills, canals and railways – are as much part of our heritage as are Roman or megalithic monuments. They remind us of a past which is not so distant, a past studied by industrial archaeologists.

The Industrial Revolution is the name given to the changes which occurred in the 18th century mainly in England and France, and in the 19th century mainly in Germany and the United States. Before this time, these were countries primarily of small towns and villages and a few large cities. The Industrial Revolution saw the introduction of mechanically powered machines which enabled existing industries to grow and new ones to emerge. In England and Wales coal, iron, steel and textile production increased; an extensive network of canals and a new railway system enabled goods to be transported throughout the country. Ports were enlarged and warehouses constructed to house both goods imported from other countries and goods awaiting export. The

▽ The Iron Bridge in Shropshire, England, was the first metal bridge in the world. It was built in 1779 using iron cast in the nearby Coalbrookdale Works. It is part of the Ironbridge Gorge open-air museum.

▷ Part of Albert Dock in Liverpool, England. The dockyard was built in 1845 and is surrounded by five-storey brick and iron warehouses. As the maritime trade decreased the once busy warehouses on the waterfront went out of use and became deserted. Recently the dock has been redeveloped, and the warehouses have been converted into shops, housing, offices and a museum. Similar changes have occurred on dockland sites in large cities throughout the world. Originally bustling, busy areas, they became derelict and rundown, but now they are once again centres of activity.

population increased considerably; towns grew, new towns appeared, and many former country folk became town dwellers. Indeed, the Industrial Revolution caused perhaps the most important changes in people's lives since ancient times. Today much evidence of early industries has been destroyed. That which remains needs to be recorded and preserved where possible.

Finding the industrial past

Industrial societies are studied by specialists with many different interests, among them historians, geographers, engineers, metallurgists and architects. Industrial archaeologists use information from these specialists to help them understand and reconstruct the industrial past. They study the physical remains of the time, for example buildings or machines, to see how they developed and changed

through the period. They can determine, too, how they were made, what was needed to make them, and how they were used. This type of information is often missing from documentary sources.

Today many areas which were once busy industrial centres no longer exist; they have been destroyed by modern development or serve purposes which may or may not reflect their past use. For example, some coalmines have been converted into museums where visitors can learn about coalmining and coalminers. The warehouses of the Albert Dock in Liverpool, England, now house a maritime museum, an art gallery, shops, offices and flats. Some railway stations, too, now serve entirely different purposes. The former Manchester Central Station, for example, is now used as an exhibition centre. Many smaller stations have disappeared or are used as ordinary houses. Railway carriages, too, have been

converted into houses or sheds for private use. Our industrial past, then, is all around us – we must learn how to spot it.

Tracking yesterday's railways

The present-day network of roads which criss-crosses most countries is busy with motor traffic carrying goods and people from one destination to another. Air traffic brings distant places together within a matter of hours. As a result rail travel, especially over very long distances, has declined. Today the rail network is not the mighty giant it was 100 years ago. Many railway lines have been closed, railway stations shut down, locomotives and carriages abandoned, and tracks overgrown. Other railway-related equipment has either disappeared or is fast disappearing.

There remains, however, a great interest in railways past and present – an interest

▷ Remains of wooden tracks excavated at the Bersham ironworks in North Wales. These were preserved because the wood had been charred (affected by burning). The earliest railways in England were made of wood and are known as waggonways. The Bersham ironworks were in use during the 17th and 18th centuries, when coal and iron ore were delivered to them by rail. Some of the original buildings have recently been excavated; they now form part of a museum heritage site at the village of Bersham.

Early railways had wooden rails attached to wooden sleepers. Evidence of these is rare because the wood usually disintegrates. This makes the discovery of the Bersham railway particularly exciting. Iron rails, which appeared towards the end of the 18th century, were fastened with metal spikes to stone sleepers set in the ground. Today, in places where the rails and spikes have been removed or reused elsewhere, stone sleeper blocks may be the only indication of a railway route.

Many early railways linked mines and quarries with canals, along which goods were transported. These lines are sometimes visible as overgrown tracks or as a small bump running across a field. Some may have been incorporated into the railway system, which was later expanded. Old maps often mark these early railways or tracks and can be a useful source for detecting them.

The changing landscape

The development of the railway system brought changes to the landscape. Tunnels were dug through hills and mountains and vast amounts of rock and earth were removed. Sometimes this was heaped up beside the railway tracks to form embankments (artificial mounds). At other times it was dumped in fields some distance away. Today these mounds appear as natural hills and the way they were originally formed has been forgotten. Some tunnels that are no longer in use may remain as holes in a hillside. A disused tunnel lies beneath the city of Edinburgh in Scotland.

Stone, brick, iron and steel viaducts and bridges built to carry trains over valleys and rivers can be found throughout Britain. Some have been reinforced with, or even replaced by, modern structures. Often the fact that one building material, for example wood, has been replaced by another, perhaps stone, gives clues to the shape or manufacture of the original structure. Many bridges and viaducts, now no longer in use, may appear as isolated monuments in the landscape.

Towns such as Swindon in England were built to house railway workers. Their houses were constructed near the railway yards and workshops. Today one of the old Swindon railway buildings is a railway museum.

which is directed mainly towards the railway locomotive. Many locomotives have been lovingly preserved in railway museums. Stories of railway lines and the trains which ran on them can be found in books and seen on videos. These are only a small part of our railway past, which is itself an important part of our industrial heritage.

The Railway Era in Britain

In Britain the period between 1830 and 1914 is sometimes referred to as the Railway Era. It was a time when railways dominated the transport system. Before this time, roads and canals had been the main means of transport. The invention of the steam engine which ran on rails laid across the landscape suddenly made travel between the countryside, town and city fast, easy and comfortable. Gradually

transportation by canal declined, becoming almost non-existent. Road travel, too, died out until the arrival of the motor car.

Looking for the evidence

The physical remains of early railways and information from documents and old maps provide a picture of the railway system in Britain during the Railway Era. Archaeological survey and excavation have shown how railways developed, and have sometimes revealed long-forgotten railways. Recent excavations of an ironworking complex at Bersham in North Wales, for example, uncovered remains of the charred rails of a wooden railway. This dates to the mid-18th century and is perhaps the earliest railway yet discovered; it was used to carry coal and iron ore to the ironworks at Bersham.

Clues and more clues

Railway stations appeared across Britain; some were quite small but those in the cities were splendid monuments to increase the prestige of railway owners. London's St Pancras Station is one such example.

Prestige was also gained by the use of crests and monograms – special emblems or symbols used to identify the companies who ran the railways. Crests and monograms may be found incorporated into parts of modern stations, on tunnel entrances and on signal boxes.

Smaller structures such as level crossings, signal boxes and mileposts are also found throughout the railway network. Stone and cast-iron mileposts may be found on abandoned lines. Cast-iron mileposts in the Forest of Dean in England, for example, date from 1815. These form just part of the wealth of evidence about the railway system.

◁ This bridge was built to go over a railway on the Isle of Wight, England. The railway is no longer in use, and the track has completely disappeared. If we did not know the story, we might wonder what the bridge was doing there.

△ A stone memorial in Otley churchyard in Yorkshire, England, was erected in memory of men who died while building a railway tunnel. The memorial is a miniature reproduction of the ornate entrance to the tunnel.

The railways and the public

Industrial archaeologists and railway historians have recorded the effects of railway construction on the landscape and the environment. But railways also affected people. They made it easier for people to travel and enabled them to take day trips to areas which would have been too far away to reach by coach and horses. To find out how railways affected people's lives, we must turn to the diaries, political reports, newspapers, paintings, sketches and songs of the period.

The development of the modern super high-speed trains has brought renewed interest to train travel. But we can still travel into the past on some of the old railway lines, which have been lovingly repaired and opened as tourist lines. As we travel, we can look for hidden clues to our great railway heritage.

SAVING OUR HERITAGE

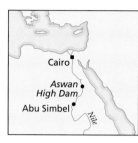

Present-day construction work often reveals traces of the past, but it can also destroy them. The vital task of documenting archaeological sites before they are lost for ever is the domain of salvage or rescue archaeology.

Changes to the land around us occur with staggering speed. Roads, railways, towns and cities are constantly being built or expanded. Archaeologists are often invited to assess an area before or during development. The developers themselves usually fund these assessments and any excavations that take place subsequently. When archaeologists have completed their salvage operations the sites are often destroyed by the modern development, although some are preserved under special conditions.

Salvage projects vary in scope from the recording of a small prehistoric campsite to the excavation of a large temple such as the Great Temple of the Aztecs in the middle of bustling Mexico City, or of a city such as Viking York in England. The Aztec temple and Viking York are now permanent museums in the modern cities. Terra Amata, a Palaeolithic camp in southern France, is a museum under an apartment block.

The most impressive salvage operation ever undertaken was the rescue of ancient monuments in Nubia, a region comprising southern Egypt and northern Sudan. Construction of the Aswan High Dam in Egypt in the 1960s caused the water level of the River Nile to rise considerably. If they had not been saved, many of the archaeological treasures of the region would have disappeared beneath the lake.

The River Nile

The Greek writer Herodotus said that Egypt was the 'gift of the Nile', whose yearly floods gave life to a barren land. From early times the floodwaters provided the irrigation necessary for crops to grow. But the floods were unpredictable: sometimes huge torrents of water caused devastation; sometimes drought brought disaster. Crops were ruined and the people suffered famine and death.

The Egyptian population has increased dramatically in the last 100 years. As a result Egypt needs a more reliable water supply to support its agriculture. In the late 19th and early 20th centuries dams were built across the Nile to store and control the floodwaters. The largest of these was the Aswan Dam, constructed in 1902 near Aswan in southern Egypt.

The Aswan High Dam

As the 20th century progressed, the water controlled by the Aswan Dam proved inadequate for the changing needs of the country. Egypt required electricity to power its new industries. Electricity can be produced cheaply using water power, but the old Aswan Dam was not large enough to produce the amount of power that was needed. Between 1960 and 1970 a huge dam, called Sudd el' Ali (popularly known as the Aswan High Dam), was built just south of the old Aswan Dam. This caused a vast lake – Lake Nasser – to form, 500 km long and between 10 km and 40 km wide.

The Sudd el' Ali enabled Egypt to develop and progress in the modern world. However, plans for its construction caused panic among governments and groups concerned with preserving world heritage sites. The area of Nubia affected by the new dam has been called an open-air museum. Many ancient monuments, churches, forts, villages and cemeteries, dating from Pharaonic times to the Middle Ages, lie along the Nile. The building of the earlier Aswan Dam had caused some of these monuments to be submerged for part of each year. Before the dam was built these temples and sites had been surveyed and recorded. The new, bigger dam would affect more temples and sites and cause many to disappear for ever under the waters of the lake. There they would eventually disintegrate and so be lost to the world. They had to be saved.

Saving the monuments

Such a salvage project was a massive and enormously expensive undertaking – one which Egypt and the Sudan could not pay for alone. The Egyptian government asked UNESCO (the United Nations Educational and Cultural Organization) to appeal to the world for money and expert help to save the Nubian monuments. Governments and individuals all around the world responded enthusiastically. Specialists from many countries worked on the project: archaeologists, pre-historians, palaeontologists,

Sites affected by the Aswan High Dam
- ● ancient site or temple
- —— old course of River Nile
- ▢ Lake Nasser

Aswan High Dam   Philae

NUBIA

Amada

Abu Simbel

0   40 km

◁ The River Nile forms an important link between Africa and the Mediterranean world. The two worlds come into contact in Nubia, an area consisting of southern Egypt and northern Sudan. The peoples who lived in the area in the past built temples, fortresses, churches, tombs, towns and settlements. This huge, open-air museum was threatened by the construction of the Aswan High Dam (Sudd el' Ali).

◁ The partially submerged temple of Trajan, one of many temples on the island of Philae, near Aswan. As the rising waters of Lake Nasser threatened to drown the temples completely, they were dismantled and re-erected on the nearby island of Agilkia.

anthropologists, Byzantine and Arabian scholars, engineers, geologists, architects and landscape artists.

At first a thorough ground and aerial survey of the area under threat was undertaken and the enormity of the problem assessed. Then followed long discussions on how best to save the temples, after which the actual salvage operation began. Most temples were cut into blocks and rebuilt in a safer place. In the case of the temple of Amada, the entire temple was placed on a platform and moved by rail to higher ground. A few temples, or parts of them, were given to museums or cities around the world in recognition of their help. Thus, there are Nubian temples in New York, Madrid, Leyden (in the Netherlands) and Berlin. The salvage project was always a race against time and the rising waters of the lake as construction of the Sudd el' Ali progressed.

The temples of Abu Simbel

The rescue of the Abu Simbel monument shows the huge scale of the operation. Built for Ramses II in the 13th century BC, it consists of a large and small temple cut

into the cliffside some 300 km south of Aswan city. The larger temple is the Pharaoh's and the smaller that of his queen, Nefertari. Four huge seated figures of Ramses II, each 20 m high, are carved into the cliff; these form the façade of his temple. Sun-rays pass through the inner halls and rooms, which are decorated with reliefs showing the Pharaoh's military campaigns. Twice a year, at the equinox, sun-rays illuminate four more statues of Egyptian gods carved into the rock at the back of the temple some 60 m behind the entrance.

Planning the rescue

For four years discussions were held and various plans proposed to save Abu Simbel, but the costs were always prohibitive. Finally, it was decided to cut the temples into blocks and re-erect them 65 m higher up the cliff. Much of the original cliff face also had to be moved to ensure that the new setting looked the same as the original. The location of the monuments added to the difficulties of the work. Abu Simbel is surrounded by water and desert and the nearest town is

1

4

5

Stages in the dismantling and reconstruction of Abu Simbel.

1 An early 19th-century drawing of Abu Simbel done about 26 years after it was discovered and when it was still partially covered with sand.

2 An aerial view of Abu Simbel showing the cofferdam built to protect it from the rising waters of Lake Nasser during salvage work.

3 The partially dismantled temple. The front of the temple was covered with sand to protect the sculptures while work progressed.

4 The head of Ramses II was removed after it had been cut away from the temple.

5 The temples of Ramses II and Nefertari in the process of being re-erected in their new location.

6 Abu Simbel today.

300 km away. Everything and everyone needed for the project had to be transported there by air or by boat. The Abu Simbel salvage project took four years to complete and cost US$ 40 million.

Work on the Aswan High Dam began in 1960, four years before work began at Abu Simbel. As the water level of the Nile rose steadily during this time, a special structure, called a cofferdam, first had to be built around the temple sites to protect them from the rising lake waters.

Cutting up the temples

Bulldozers and pneumatic tools were used to remove hundreds of tons of cliff rock above the temples. When most of the rock had been taken away, a scaffolding was erected in the inner rooms to prevent the temples from collapsing. The entire monument was then filled and covered with sand to protect it. Next the rock of the temples themselves was cut into blocks weighing between 20 and 30 tons.

Workers tried different methods to cut the rock into blocks. They discovered that saws were the most suitable tools. But the edges wore down so rapidly that the saws had to be fitted with special teeth made of hard metal. The workers used motorized chain-saws to cut into the back of the block until they were close to the sculptured surface. They did the crucial final cutting from the front of the block, using specially made fine hand-saws.

There was a danger that some of the

3

6

stone in the temples would break during the cutting process. To avoid this, the weaker blocks were strengthened with steel bars and a special type of glue.

The temples were cut into 1042 huge blocks. Holes were drilled in them and special steel lifting bars were fitted. These were attached to cranes that lifted them away from the rock-face. The blocks were then carefully moved to a storage area, where specialists inspected them and carried out restoration work.

Re-erecting the temples

The temples were re-erected at the top of the hill from which they had been cut. When the new foundations had been carefully prepared, the blocks were replaced in their correct positions and made firm with concrete. A huge concrete dome was then built over each temple. Artificial hills, made from the rock that had been excavated from the cliff, were subsequently constructed over

and behind the dome. In this way the Abu Simbel temples were once more placed in a cliff setting, in exactly the same positions and facing in the same direction as at the original site.

As we look at the temples today, we can only marvel at the astounding ability of the ancient Egyptians to create such monuments. We also marvel at the phenomenal modern technology which moved those same monuments into a new position over 3000 years later.

ETHNOARCHAEOLOGY

Ethnoarchaeology is the study of living groups of people from an archaeological point of view. Careful observation of this sort can sometimes help archaeologists understand evidence of past societies revealed during excavations.

During the 19th and early 20th centuries researchers began to study how the descendants of the original inhabitants of a country lived. The study of these aboriginal peoples is called ethnography. At first these groups were believed to be living examples of prehistoric peoples, and their way of life to be a reflection of prehistoric life. However, we now know that modern aboriginal life is not exactly the same as ancient life. Nevertheless, ethnographic studies do provide us with a range of situations we can observe in order to help us to understand the past more clearly. They cannot, of course, tell us everything we might wish to know about the vanished peoples of the past.

Ethnoarchaeologists work as ethnographers. They usually live with a group

of people, observing and recording their daily life. They look for evidence that might survive for future archaeologists to find, and study how that evidence relates to the actual activities and behaviour of the group. This approach has been used, for example, to study pottery making, farming techniques, steel making and hunting practices.

Stone tool patterning in Palaeolithic sites in France

In 1967 Lewis Binford, an American archaeologist, studied the finds from a number of sites belonging to the Middle Palaeolithic (a period between about 200,000 and 50,000 years ago) in the Dordogne region of France. Thousands of stone tools, bone fragments and hearths had been revealed during years of excavations. But the pattern of remains was not always the same at each site.

Archaeologists proposed rival theories to account for the variation in stone tools and bone remains. François Bordes, a French archaeologist, believed that different types of stone tools belonged to different tribes of people. Lewis Binford believed that the sites could have been

occupied by the same tribe and that the differences were due to the variety of activities carried out at the site.

Enter ethnoarchaeology

As Palaeolithic groups hunted animals and gathered plants for food, Binford decided to study a group of modern hunter-gatherers. He wanted to see how they moved from camp to camp, how they

△ Hot-climate shelters made from grasses and used by the San Bushmen of southern Africa. Future archaeologists would find little evidence of such shelters.

hunted, how they made, used and discarded stone tools, and what they did with bones. He felt an ethnoarchaeological approach might help him understand how archaeological sites can be formed and what the different patterns of stone tools and bones at Palaeolithic sites might mean. To do this, he spent periods between 1969 and 1973 with the Nunamiut Inuits in northern Alaska.

Why did Binford choose Inuits? Why not Australian aboriginal peoples or southern African San Bushmen, who sometimes lead a hunting and gathering way of life? Binford saw similarities between French Palaeolithic and Inuit groups: both lived by hunting and on occasion even hunted the same animal, reindeer (called caribou in Alaska). In addition, the present-day environment in Alaska possibly resembles that of the cold periods which dominated Europe during much of the Middle Palaeolithic.

Nunamiut life

Binford studied the activities of a group of 30 to 40 Nunamiut. He discovered that during their lifetime they travelled over an immense territory, much larger than people had previously realized. They did not exploit the entire territory at any one time; they stayed in one place until the wood, animal and plant resources began

◁ Australian aboriginal hunters using spear throwers. The long spear is linked to an attachment (the thrower), which propels the spear much further than the hunter could normally achieve. Ethnoarchaeological observation shows how spear throwers found on Palaeolithic sites were used.

▷ Lewis Binford plotted on a map the campsites used by a Nunamiut family in one year. It shows that they travelled widely in search of food, staying for periods of between two days and seven months (the winter) in a camp. Palaeolithic hunters may have moved long distances too.

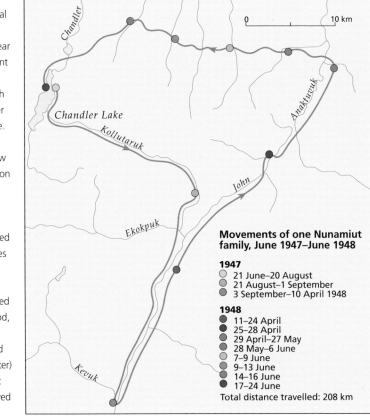

Movements of one Nunamiut family, June 1947–June 1948

1947
○ 21 June–20 August
○ 21 August–1 September
○ 3 September–10 April 1948

1948
● 11–24 April
● 25–28 April
● 29 April–27 May
● 28 May–6 June
○ 7–9 June
● 9–13 June
● 14–16 June
● 17–24 June

Total distance travelled: 208 km

to dwindle and then moved to another region. In this way the plants and animals did not disappear entirely but had time to regenerate.

As they moved around the land the Nunamiut set up camp for a few days or some months, depending on what they wanted to do – hunt caribou, fish at a good spot, or stay for the winter. An archaeologist studying this area in the future could therefore expect to find evidence of many short-term, seasonal camps around the landscape. But these would be the camps of one group not of many different groups.

As they travelled around, the Nunamiut sometimes camped in new places but they often returned to campsites used in previous years. The potential archaeological evidence at some camps would therefore be a mixture of remains from several visits to the same site. At other sites it would represent one occupation by the hunters. Reused campsites are larger than

single visit sites, with more signs of tents, stones, bones and hearths. An archaeologist might think that large sites had been occupied by many people rather than a few hunters returning to the same campsite.

A variety of campsites

Binford studied some Nunamiut sites associated with the hunting of caribou. These sites included a hunting camp, a place where animals were killed and butchered, and a number of stone-lined pits that were used to store meat. The sites were not always near each other, although they were all used during the same period by one group of hunters. Because different activities took place at these sites, the pattern of evidence which archaeologists would see is different. Circles of stones seen at the hunting campsite, for example, were used to secure caribou skins while they were

drying. At the butchering area of the kill site the hunter placed the dead caribou on the ground and worked around it as he removed the skin and cut the meat. He threw the waste and bones away behind him as he worked. When he had finished he removed the meat, leaving a ring of discarded bones surrounding a relatively clear area where the animal carcass had been.

At a third site, a large stone structure was made to store food. On an archaeological site such evidence might be interpreted as a house rather than a food storage area. Binford notes that structures on some Russian Palaeolithic sites which have been called 'pit houses' may in fact have been storage pits associated with butchery sites.

▽ An Inuit hunter in the winter. The cold conditions of Alaska can give us an idea of Ice Age conditions. People may have worn animal-skin clothes to keep warm in the bitterly cold winters.

Difficulties of interpretation

Binford also saw traps, surrounded by small stone walls, which were made to catch animals or protect stored meat. He feels that many such traps are visible on archaeological sites but that they are often interpreted as storage pits or ritual areas, never as animal traps.

He watched a family of hunters kill 50 caribou at one site. The processing of the meat took 12 days. The family then moved on but left behind them an enormous amount of bones. An archaeologist studying the site might think that a large group had lived there for a long time, perhaps not considering that bones are not always the result of meals.

Binford's study demonstrates that evidence at the Nunamiut sites could reflect a variety of activities. These activities are not always easy to identify. It is impossible to identify from archaeological evidence everything which took place on a Palaeolithic site. But archaeologists must be aware of the range of possible activities which may occur in order to try and discover the function of the site.

Around the campfire

Campfires or hearths are often busy areas: people prepare and eat food, make and repair tools, or just chatter. Can we see evidence of these activities on archaeological sites? Binford noted that the Nunamiut often ate their meals sitting around the hearth outside their tents. They dropped the small bones in or near the fire, but tossed the larger bones behind them. Sometimes someone dumped a mass of bones and bone splinters from the soup pot on the ground near the fire.

When Binford mapped the remains three different patterns could be seen: a small circle of bones near the hearth, a larger circle of bones further away from the hearth and a small dump of bone splinters on one side. Similar patterns of remains have been found in many Palaeolithic sites.

Patterns of discard around a hearth inside a tent are different. People do not throw bones behind them because it would be too untidy in the confined space of a tent. As a result of his ethnoarchaeological studies, Binford believes that the

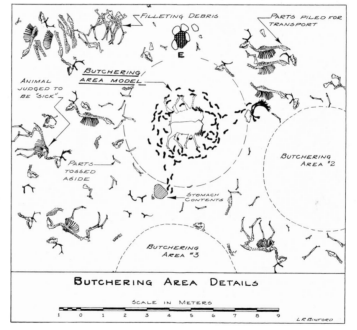

△ Part of an area where Nunamiut hunters had butchered caribou (see plan to the left). The central area, free of bones, is where the animal was placed. The hunters threw the waste pieces behind them.

◁ Plan of a caribou butchery area. The Nunamiut hunters walked around the animal as they cut it into pieces. Parts of the animal were placed on one side to be taken away. Other parts were tossed aside.

pattern of waste seen around some of the hearths at the later Palaeolithic site of Pincevent in northern France shows that the hunters sat around an open-air hearth and not inside a tent, as the excavator of the site had originally suggested.

In his later work, Binford studied the role carnivores played in accumulating bones. He also looked at carnivore tooth marks on bones, which archaeologists might wrongly interpret as evidence for human hunting and butchery of animal carcasses with stone tools.

Lewis Binford has demonstrated how studying the life of modern groups of people such as hunters and gatherers can help archaeologists understand the remains uncovered during excavation. He has shown how important it is to understand site formation processes – the way archaeological sites are formed – and how different they can be. Ethnoarchaeology can certainly help us in our quest to understand more about past ways of life, although it will never allow us to decode all the secrets of an excavated site.

THE ARCHAEOLOGY OF TODAY

Archaeologists learn much about past societies from their rubbish. Garbage archaeologists learn about our own society by studying our refuse.

Rubbish is important in archaeology because it contains evidence of everyday life. Garbage archaeology – the study of rubbish – is the most recent branch of archaeology. It is called garbage archaeology, or garbology, because it is done predominantly in the United States of America, where rubbish is often known as garbage.

The Garbage Project

In 1973 Professor William Rathje and a group of his students from the University of Arizona undertook a project to look at the garbage from households in the city of Tucson. This was called the Garbage Project. It has since expanded to cover many other American cities plus Mexico City as well. The project uses archaeological techniques to study modern garbage

in order to gain a more accurate picture of modern life. Since 1973, hundreds of tons of garbage have been studied.

Today, the Garbage Project has a database of information on most aspects of modern American life. This can tell us about what people eat, how much they waste and what they do during a food shortage. It provides information about the type and quantity of hazardous materials that people throw away and the different buying patterns of rich and poor households. It has also revealed differences between what people say they eat and do and what actually turns up in their rubbish.

Processing the garbage

The Garbage Project cannot look at all the garbage from every household in a city. Houses are selected at random from

various city neighbourhoods. Their garbage is then collected regularly over a period of time and delivered to the project processing site.

The Garbage Project is based in a large, partially covered building on the University of Arizona campus. Garbage is stored in freezers to lessen the smell, prevent maggots from developing, and keep flies away.

When bags of garbage are removed from the freezers, volunteer college students, dressed in protective clothing, quickly sort through it. Items are sorted into a number of specific categories such as food, household items, hazardous materials and personal items. Detailed information on each item is then carefully recorded on a form and entered into a computer. Once the garbage has been studied and recorded, it is taken away to the city dump.

Reaction to food shortages

Garbage studies have produced revealing insights into human behaviour patterns related to food. One such pattern concerns food shortages. In the spring of 1973 there was a beef shortage in the United States. The Garbage Project compared the amount of meat people threw away at this time with the amount they discarded when meat was plentiful. It is fairly easy to collect data on meat and other products

△ Garbage archaeologists sort out garbage and record the items on special recording sheets, just as other archaeologists sort and record the objects found in excavation. However, garbage archaeologists wear protective clothing, including a mask when necessary.

◁ Most of us would not be happy sitting on a smelly rubbish dump, but Professor William Rathje's study of modern rubbish shows that we can learn much about ourselves from the things we throw away. His work is also helping local governments in the USA to discover what changes occur to rubbish in a dump and how long it takes to decompose.

bought in a supermarket. The product, weight, price and date are usually marked on the package. Data on beef was collected for 15 months.

The results showed that people wasted more beef when it was in short supply. Professor Rathje and his team suggested that people had resorted to 'crisis buying', purchasing lots of meat when it was available. But they did not always have enough space to store the extra meat and had to discard it when it began to go off. They also bought cuts of meat which they did

not usually buy and did not know how to cook properly. Consequently these often ended up in the rubbish bin.

In the spring of 1975 there was a shortage of sugar in the United States. However, there was no shortage in Mexico, which is not far from Tucson, the Garbage Project's home base. So Tucson shoppers bought Mexican sugar. But Mexican sugar is less refined than American sugar – it is brown and hardens quickly. Soon brown lumps of sugar were found in the Tucson garbage. Sugar

substitutes, too, began to make an increased appearance in waste bins.

On the basis of their findings, the Garbage Project team suggested that food items which are eaten on a regular basis are not wasted as much as more exotic food items. Bread is a good example. They found that special breads such as muffins, bagels and rolls are thrown away more often than standard, sliced bread. Sliced bread is used every day for sandwiches, while other breads might be bought for special occasions. If speciality breads are

HAZARDOUS WASTE

Hazardous waste includes motor oil, oil-based paints, stains and varnishes, pesticides, chemicals and similar products. The Garbage Project team wanted to discover how much was thrown away. They studied hazardous waste from a number of American cities. It formed only a small amount of each household's garbage. But when hazardous waste from all households is deposited in the city dump, it may pose a significant health risk.

The study also revealed that types of hazardous product differed from one neighbourhood to another. Car items such as motor oil and lubricants were found most often in the garbage from low-income areas. Middle-income neighbourhoods seemed to be concerned with home improvements as well: their waste included items such as paints, varnishes and stains. Garden products, such as herbicides and fertilizers, were found more in the garbage from affluent areas.

△ A sample of car-related hazardous waste found in garbage bins. The Garbage Project study found that 1 per cent of all household rubbish consisted of hazardous waste – not much from one household but a huge amount when we consider all the households in a city or country.

▷ This chart shows the amounts and types of hazardous waste collected from low-income, middle-income and affluent areas. People do not usually know what types of hazardous waste they throw away.

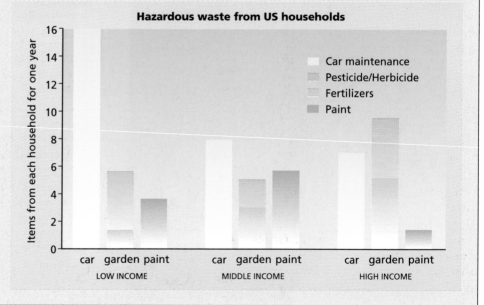

Hazardous waste from US households

Items from each household for one year

- Car maintenance
- Pesticide/Herbicide
- Fertilizers
- Paint

car garden paint   car garden paint   car garden paint
LOW INCOME   MIDDLE INCOME   HIGH INCOME

not eaten fairly quickly, they may be put to one side and forgotten. Eventually they will go stale and have to be thrown away.

Fatty issues

For many years the project collected data about the amount of fat trimmed off meat. There was little change in the amount of fat trimmings found in garbage collected between 1976 and 1982. From 1983 onwards the amount doubled and it remains high today. Why did people begin to discard greater quantities of fat? After 1982 the health risk caused by the consumption of fat, especially that from red meats, was highly publicized. As a result consumers sensibly bought less red meat and cut off more fat. However, they also bought more processed meat, such as hot dogs, salami, bacon and sausages. These processed meats have a much higher fat content than fresh meat, so the health risk still remains.

Rich and poor

Another of the Garbage Project's studies compared buying patterns in low-income and higher-income areas in two American cities. The results showed that poorer people usually bought small packets of food and other household products. Large, economy-size packets tended to be found in the rubbish in more affluent neighbourhoods. People with low incomes cannot afford to pay the extra money for economy-size packets, although large packets last much longer than small ones and are more economical in the long run.

Interviews

The Garbage Project uses two main methods of data collection. The principal method is picking up garbage from houses in different city areas and studying it. The second method consists of interviews with householders about the rubbish they throw away. This allows the contents of the garbage bin to be compared with what people say they throw away. The results are surprising. What people claim to have used and thrown away does not usually match what is found in their rubbish.

More food is always found in bins than people say they have thrown away. Perhaps they do not wish to appear wasteful when questioned about how much food they throw away. The stress on eating healthy food is reflected in interviews but not in the garbage. People claim they eat more healthy food than junk or fattening food. The less healthy products found in the garbage tell a different story.

Householders do not usually lie deliberately when interviewed. They know that the evidence is in their garbage. They are just not aware of exactly what they throw away. In contrast, they provide much more accurate information on what other people in the house consume.

What can we learn from the Garbage Project?

Archaeologists traditionally study the rubbish of ancient societies in order to help them understand how people lived.

The Garbage Project demonstrates that the same can be done with modern refuse. It can provide an accurate picture of groups of people by looking at what they throw away.

We may think that in this modern age we do not need to look at rubbish to learn about ourselves. The Garbage Project studies have shown this to be false. They have shown that some of our ideas about the way people behave are incorrect. For example, people tend to waste more food in times of shortage.

Garbage archaeology is a young but important branch of modern archaeology. We may shudder when we think of picking through mounds of mushy, smelly garbage, but it is surely the archaeology of today.

▽ Contents of a modern dustbin in London, England. What does it tell us about the way of life of the family who threw it away?

LEARNING FROM THE PAST

Painted walls, written words and clay pots hold much more information than we see. The hands that produced them belonged to people who, like us, had happy and sad times and who held their own beliefs about life and death. Burial customs, too, involve more than just the disposal of a dead body. Through archaeology we can look beyond the outward appearance of the evidence to try to understand the inner meaning that it holds.

ARTISTS OF THE PAST

For 40,000 years people have used painting and sculpture as a way to express their beliefs, thoughts and feelings. While archaeologists can determine how and when past artists worked, it is more difficult to discover what was in their minds.

In December 1994 archaeologist Jean-Marie Chauvet and two friends made the find of a lifetime. They discovered a cave 500 m underground in the Ardèche region of south-west France. The cave walls were covered with paintings and engravings estimated to be between 17,000 and 20,000 years old. Chauvet and his companions were the first humans to enter the cave since the last artists left, thousands of years before.

The galleries of this newly found archaeological treasure, now named Chauvet Cave, are hundreds of metres long. Among the variety of Ice Age animals displayed on the walls are horses, rhinoceros, lions, bison, aurochs (wild oxen), bears, mammoths, ibex (wild goats), a panther and owls. Some are shown fighting, others walking. There are also mysterious groups of painted dots, lines and handprints.

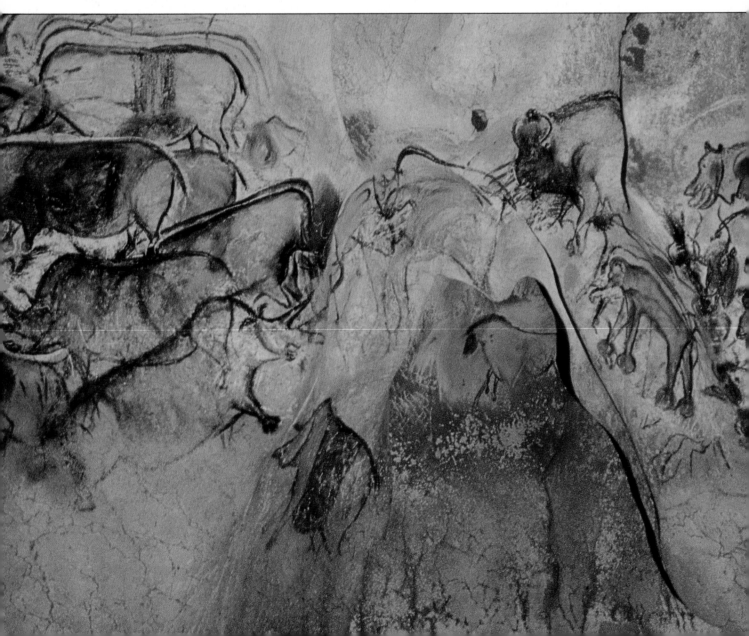

Palaeolithic artists were not the only living creatures to use Chauvet Cave. The remains of more than 100 cave bears litter the galleries. Some skeletons lie where the animals died during hibernation; other bones had been moved to one side by the painters as they went through the cave. One bear skull had been deliberately placed on a rock in the centre of a gallery. It seems unlikely that humans and bears occupied the cave at the same time, as it would have been far too dangerous.

Further evidence of the artists lies on the floor of the cave: stone tools, stone lamps and hearths as well as numerous human and bear footprints. Future study of the footprints should indicate when animals and humans occupied the cave. It may well reveal if the people walked, ran or danced in the cave and whether these people were old, young, male or female.

◁ Part of the painted wall of the recently discovered Chauvet Cave. Unlike other large cave art sites, many dangerous animals are shown on the walls of Chauvet Cave, among them woolly rhinoceros and panthers.

△ ▷ Small female statuettes called 'Venus figurines' in limestone (left) and mammoth ivory (right). Found widely and dating to between 25,000 and 12,000 years ago, they were once (but are no longer) believed to be symbols of fertility.

The beginning of Palaeolithic art

The first cave paintings occurred about 20,000 years ago, but the earliest clear signs of art appeared in Europe about 20,000 years before this, during a period known as the Upper Palaeolithic. The artists were the first truly modern humans, *Homo sapiens sapiens*. The earliest art consisted of numerous pieces of what archaeologists call portable art: superb sculptures and engravings on bone, antler, ivory, wood, amber and stone, as well as personal ornaments such as pendants and necklaces made from pierced animal teeth, shells and ivory beads.

Portable art is found over a wide geographic area from northern Africa to Siberia. Among the more famous objects are the often enormously fat female forms called 'Venus figurines'. Their faces are not clearly defined but their hairstyles – or perhaps headdresses – are often shown. Some of these exquisite sculptures (such as the head on page 132) are only a few centimetres tall.

The mystery of caves

While portable art was widespread, the painted cave sites in Europe, of which there are over 200, are located mainly in south-west France and northern Spain. Some, such as Niaux in France and Altamira in Spain, have galleries hundreds of metres long which penetrate deep inside the cave. Like Chauvet Cave, these contain hundreds of paintings and engravings.

The huge spectacular cave sites have provided the world with breathtakingly beautiful art. Large Ice Age animals predominate, but smaller animals such as hares, birds, fish and reptiles appear too, although infrequently. Humans are rarely shown; among those depicted some seem to be wearing masks, animal skins and antlers. This may be camouflage for hunting purposes or for use in ritual ceremonies, but we cannot be sure. As in Chauvet Cave, dots, lines and handprints are often found on cave walls. Some researchers suggest that the dots and lines are a form of counting.

Animal forms have been found partially sculpted out of walls. Perhaps the most impressive are the 2 m-long clay bison in the cave of Le Tuc d'Audoubert,

and the line of ten lifesize horses on the rock overhang at Cap Blanc, both in south-west France.

Most wall art is found along the corridors and chambers of cave systems, often in places which are extremely difficult to reach. A narrow corridor at the back of the Altamira cave is crowded with paintings of bison, ibex, horses, reindeer, mammoths and boars, as well as lines and dots. The galleries approaching this corridor are also covered with paintings. Altamira is famous for the spectacular ceiling in one of its side chambers; it is covered with paintings of near lifesize animals, mainly bison.

What do the paintings mean?

We will never know for sure what the paintings meant to the artists who created them and the people who saw them so many thousands of years ago. Many explanations have been proposed. One suggestion is that people liked to decorate their homes much as we decorate our homes today; another is that they painted because they liked painting. These explanations seem unlikely. Most paintings are in dark – and often almost inaccessible – caves, which would never

△ Spotted horses and handprints from the French cave of Pech Merle. Handprints are found not only in French Palaeolithic art but also in Australian aboriginal art. Paintings on cave walls may have been done over thousands of years, and it is common to find animals painted on top of other animals.

▷ About 12,000 years ago three children walked barefoot into Niaux Cave in France. Human footprints found inside many caves show that adults and children were not afraid to go into the dark caves. The footprints never show signs of frostbite, indicating that it was not freezing inside the caves during the last Ice Age.

PALAEOLITHIC ARTISTS AT WORK

Much cave art is in total darkness. The artists would have needed light in order to create their masterpieces. Archaeologists have found stone lamps – lumps of stone hollowed in the centre which were filled with animal fat. The remains of hearths show that firelight, too, was used to illuminate working areas.

Cave artists ground their paints from minerals such as ochre, which gave red, brown and yellow, and manganese oxide, which produced black and violet. There are no blues or greens in Palaeolithic art. Mineral fragments and the implements used to grind them have been found in Lascaux Cave in south-west France. Grinding stones are often stained with the colour of the powdered pigment. A few containers with mixtures of powdered minerals show that the painters experimented with colour.

Lumps of coloured pigments found at a few sites have been interpreted by some archaeologists as painting crayons. Animal hair or vegetable fibres could have been used as brushes, but none have been found. Artists sometimes marked the soft surfaces of walls with their fingers. Experiments demonstrate that hand stencils are best produced by spitting powder on to and around the hands. Stone tools, found at many sites, would have been used for engraving.

Cave paintings are sometimes found high up on the cave walls or ceilings, beyond the reach of humans. Evidence of post holes in some sites indicates that artists erected scaffolding in order to paint these areas. The scaffolds were either removed or have disintegrated over time.

▷ A limestone lamp found in Lascaux Cave in France. Artists would never have seen their work in bright light.

have been fully illuminated by fires and lamps. Other archaeologists have seen the paintings as 'sympathetic' hunting magic: the artists hoped that painting the animals they wanted to catch would bring them success in the hunt.

Recently it has been suggested that the well-sheltered environments of south-west France and northern Spain were more densely populated than other areas during the coldest period of the last Ice Age. Cave sites, especially the large ones such as Lascaux, Altamira and possibly Chauvet, may have been centres where people met for particular ceremonies: perhaps to arrange marriages, to initiate boys and girls into adolescence, to settle arguments, to define hunting areas, to make alliances or to appease the gods. Another suggestion is that sites may have been controlled by tribal chiefs who used them as a display of power. We do not know, but the discovery of Chauvet Cave may help answer some of the questions.

LEARNING FROM ROCK PAINTINGS

We cannot look at modern European rock paintings in order to attempt to understand Palaeolithic art. Modern Europeans do not paint caves as their Palaeolithic ancestors did. In some parts of the world, however, rock painting has a long history which has continued to the present day, or until recent times. The art of Australian aboriginal peoples and southern African San peoples has increased our appreciation of these art traditions, and has perhaps made us more aware of possible interpretations of Palaeolithic art.

Australian artists

Australian aboriginal art has a long history, stretching back as much as 20,000 and possibly 40,000 years. Some present-day aboriginal peoples continue traditional painting. Although they paint mostly on bark, until recently many painted on rock faces. Researchers have discovered much about aboriginal art by speaking to the artists. Most Australian rock art is associated with religious myths, beliefs and ceremonies. It is often linked to what the aboriginal people call 'the Dreamtime' – the time when ancestral beings created the world.

There are thousands of rock art sites in Australia. Arnhem Land in the Northern Territory has over 10,000 sites. Many of

◁ A painted rock shelter in Arnhem Land, Australia. Hand stencils are common in aboriginal paintings. Modern aboriginal people have explained that some hand stencils are the mark of the artist or the sign of a visitor to the cave.

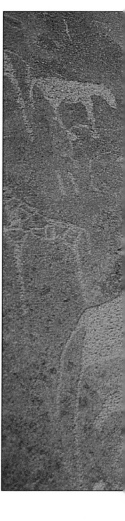

these have been visited time and time again and have hundreds of paintings dating from the Ice Age to recent times.

The painted rock shelters of Arnhem Land

The earliest paintings show freshwater fish, land animals and birds – kangaroos, wallabies, emus and animals now extinct such as the Tasmanian tiger. There are no paintings of sea fish or sea animals. The presence of animals usually found further inland suggests that the sea was further away at that time than it is today.

People are often shown wearing ornaments on their heads, arms or necks. Some figures have human bodies with animal heads. There are also narrative scenes that tell a story – scenes of people hunting and dancing. Modern-day aboriginal peoples do not know who created these paintings but attribute them to the 'Mimi' spirits – people who are invisible and who live in the rocks.

Engravings of circles, lines, dots, animal and bird tracks are found on many rock faces throughout Australia, as are painted hand stencils.

The end of the Ice Age brought a change in the Australian environment;

this is mirrored in the rock art. Paintings of sea fish and crocodiles became common. The style of art also changed to one known as x-ray, in which the outside and inside organs of the animals are depicted. Some researchers believe this symbolizes the wealth of food available but others maintain that it indicates tribal use of the land.

▷ Engravings of animals on a rock face in southern Africa. The engravings of animals, which are easily recognizable, were done by southern African San peoples more than 3000 years ago.

◁ Part of a painted rock shelter at Ingaladdi, Australia. Artists often paint on the same rock, even if they have to paint over older figures. They also regularly add colour to rock paintings to honour their ancestors and the spirits of the Dreamtime.

The most recent phase of Arnhem Land art shows the arrival of European settlers and Macassan fishermen from Indonesia. This contact is documented on the rock faces, where boats, ships, horses and guns are depicted.

Modern aboriginal peoples regularly add colour to rock paintings, especially the 'Mimi' figures, in honour of their ancestors and the spirits of the Dreamtime.

The hidden meaning of southern African rock art

Rock painting in southern Africa began 20,000 years ago and continued until the 19th century. Unlike European Palaeolithic cave paintings, the southern African paintings tend to be on rock faces exposed to the sun. For a long time people believed the paintings showed historical events and scenes of everyday life such as dancing, hunting and religious ceremonies, and in some cases this seems to have been correct.

More recently a South African archaeologist, Dr Lewis-Williams, began to study the paintings more carefully. He noticed that certain similar details were found in pictures over a wide area. Some animals, especially the eland (a type of antelope), appear more regularly than others. Lines are often drawn coming from the nose, arms, head or spine of people and animals. Sometimes lines curve around animals or a row of short, straight lines sticks up from their backs. Many people are bent over, arms stretched out behind them, or supporting themselves with two sticks. Some figures are part human and part animal.

The power of trance

In order to try and understand the paintings, Lewis-Williams turned to 19th-century documents in which the San spoke about their myths, beliefs and art. Shamen (medicine men) were an important part of San society. It was believed that their magic could bring success to the hunt, make rain and cure the sick. During a dance ceremony shamen fell into a state of trance, when they performed their magic.

San accounts of their life indicate that many of the details Lewis-Williams noticed in the paintings were related to shamen and the trance dance. People in a trance bend over and their arms stretch backwards; sometimes they need the support of sticks to stop them falling down. Lines from the body may show the shaman's power entering or leaving his body, sickness being expelled, or the sweating which occurs during a trance. Lines from noses are nosebleeds, which happen when people are in a trance. Dying animals have nosebleeds and the hairs on their spines stand on end.

While some of the rock art in southern Africa shows scenes of everyday life, Lewis-Williams's research demonstrates the importance of religious ritual in San life. An understanding of such aspects of southern African rock art and the art of the Australian aboriginal peoples may perhaps help us to unravel some of the secrets of Palaeolithic art. But we will never understand the whole story.

◁ San men dance around a shaman and a sick person. The rhythm of the dance ceremony causes the shaman to fall into a trance when he performs his curing magic.

KNOW THEM BY THEIR WRITINGS

Through their writings people provide insights into themselves and their way of life. These documents are a valuable resource for archaeologists and reveal much of the past which might otherwise be lost to us.

Writing first developed more than 5000 years ago in ancient Mesopotamia, an area lying mainly within what is now Iraq. More specifically, it emerged in that part of southern Mesopotamia known as Sumer. Other forms of writing evolved slightly later, among them Egyptian, Indus and Chinese. Although the Egyptians and Indus peoples may have got the idea of writing from Mesopotamian merchants with whom they traded goods, their scripts are different. Chinese and the more recent Mesoamerican writing developed independently.

Although writing provides a direct link with people from the past, the archaeologist cannot accept that everything written is true. Accounting records may be correct, but stories or epics relating historical events may not be entirely true. For example, in order to emphasize their importance rulers often instructed scribes

◁ Part of the Egyptian Book of the Dead written in hieroglyphics on papyrus and buried with the mummy of the scribe Ani. It is a collection of spells and instructions which were thought to help dead people on their voyage to the afterlife. The body is shown being carried on a boat over the river of death to the afterlife. But it first had to pass through the dangerous underworld, and it was assisted in this by the information in the Book of the Dead. Four jars containing the liver, lungs, intestines and stomach of the deceased are placed below the mummy on the boat.

to write flattering words about their magnificent deeds. We never find a ruler ordering inscriptions to be made about battles he has lost or crimes he may have committed. Nevertheless the wary archaeologist can gain a great deal of information from written documents.

The pathway to writing in Mesopotamia

Many Mesopotamian documents have survived because they were written on wet clay which was dried in the sun or hardened by fire. As a result, archaeologists and palaeographers (those who study ancient scripts) have been able to trace accurately the development of Sumerian script.

Keeping accounts with clay

Early counting systems took the form of small, geometrically shaped clay tokens. These have been found on sites in northern Mesopotamia dating to about 8000 years ago. Archaeologists believe that initially each token represented one unspecified item. Some tokens have holes through them, perhaps so that they could be strung together to indicate a number of items. Later, the shape of a token began to represent a particular item (one token for sheep, for example), while token size indicated the amount (small for one, large for more than one). These tokens were placed in a bag and sent with goods that were being traded. They thus formed a record: on arrival the goods and tokens could be compared to ensure that they agreed.

Later still, tokens were placed inside a clay ball, called a 'bulla'. This was then closed and stamped with a seal. In time token shapes were impressed or incised on the outside of the ball. Incising was done with a reed pen called a stylus, which would have been pointed at one end and round at the other. The balls had to be broken to retrieve the tokens.

Numerous tokens and broken balls, as well as a few intact balls, have been found. However, modern x-ray techniques, used to reveal the contents of intact balls, show that token shapes on the outside do not always match the tokens inside the balls.

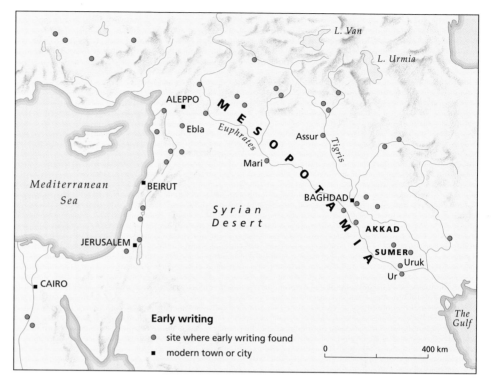

△ Map of ancient Mesopotamia and the eastern Mediterranean showing some of the sites where evidence of early written documents has been recovered during archaeological excavations.

◁ A clay 'bulla' and clay tokens from Mesopotamia. Tokens were placed in the bulla as a way of keeping records. The impression of a cylinder seal can be seen on the outside of the bulla.

STONE SEALS ON CLAY

Cylinder seals are small, cylindrical pieces of stone on which a design was carved. As the cylinder was rolled across soft clay it left repeated impressions of the design. Each seal was different, belonging to one person who used it as a stamp, a guarantee of goods, a trade mark or a badge of office.

Seals were used to close all types of container: jars, bags, clay balls or even rooms. It was easy, therefore, to discover if containers had been tampered with or opened unlawfully.

◁ A cylinder seal (Assyrian, about 800 BC) and the impression it leaves when rolled over wet clay.

more words to be placed on the small space of a clay tablet. As cuneiform signs represented sounds they could be used to write any language. Consequently cuneiform became the common form of writing throughout the ancient Near East, from ancient Turkey to Iran to the Levant (the eastern Mediterranean).

Most of the nearly 5000 cuneiform tablets found at Uruk and the majority of documents found elsewhere in the ancient Near East deal with numbers and goods: they are accounts. However, there were also a few lists of birds, animals, trees, vessels and professions. When no longer needed the document was thrown away. Gradually writing included a wider range of topics: historical (king lists, wars, treaties, alliances), epic stories and poems, teaching texts, dictionaries, scientific texts, medical texts, law codes, zoological texts and many more.

Learning to be a scribe

Cuneiform was a difficult script to master. Consequently most of the population, including kings and ministers, were illiterate. Students spent many hard years at school studying mathematics and surveying, as well as learning how to read and write cuneiform. Teaching tablets have been found with lists of names, which students had to copy. Some tablets have the teacher's work on one side and the student's copy on the reverse. We know that discipline was strict and that there were several beatings for the slightest offence. But in the end scribes could become powerful, as they were the only people who were able to understand and translate written information.

THE DEVELOPMENT OF CUNEIFORM

Clay balls are rather clumsy to carry and inconvenient to use. By about 3200 BC they had been replaced by square or rectangular clay tablets on to which symbols and pictures representing numbers and objects were impressed. The earliest tablets were found at Uruk, a Sumerian city with a population of about 50,000 people. Until this time writing had been pictographic – a picture represented an object. The picture then came to represent not only the object but the sound too. As a result, sounds could be used to build up words which could not be shown as a picture, for example 'difficult' or 'boring'.

About 3100 BC the shape of styli changed: the round end was replaced by a triangular one and signs were impressed, not incised as with the pencil-shaped styli, leaving wedge-shaped marks in the wet clay. The shape of signs altered, too: most became less like pictures, gradually taking the form

of writing known as 'cuneiform' (*cuneus* means wedge in Latin). The introduction of the new cuneiform signs allowed many

◁ A cuneiform clay tablet from Sumer dating to about 2900 BC. It lists field sizes and crops.

The library at Ebla

In the mid-1970s Italian archaeologists excavating in the ancient city of Ebla in Syria discovered a palace library with about 20,000 clay tablets and fragments. The cuneiform tablets (dating to about 2300 BC) were written in Eblaite, a previously unknown language. They dealt with the final 150 years of the city, before it was destroyed by enemy forces. In a room near the library the scribes' writing tools were found: a jar full of clay, bone styli and stone erasers.

The information in these tablets showed that Ebla was a much more powerful state than archaeologists had imagined. Most of the texts are administrative records relating to farming (storage and distribution of grain) and industry (working of metals, textiles, wood and precious stones). They also indicate international trade: Ebla had contacts with more than 80 kingdoms, many of which have never been located. It was an extremely rich city which amassed tons of silver and gold from trade and tribute. It also attracted many visitors: kings, ambassadors, businessmen, singers and skilled artisans.

Correspondence in clay

Letters were written in different languages in cuneiform, although for a long time international, diplomatic correspondence was in Akkadian (Akkad was a region to the north of Sumer). Some letters cover diplomatic matters, royal marriages and gifts exchanged between states. Others give us a glimpse of more personal matters. One example is the private correspondence between Shamshi-Adad, king of Assyria, and his sons. Between 1810 and 1760 BC the city of Mari was under Assyrian control. As Mari was far away the king sent one of his sons, Yasmah-Adad, to govern it for him. But Yasmah-Adad was lazy and received many angry letters from his father: 'As to you, how long will it be necessary for us continually to guide you? How much longer will you be unable to administer your own house? Do you not see your own brother commanding far-flung armies?' We can understand Shamshi-Adad's irritation and imagine Yasmah-Adad's reaction to the letter.

△ Chinese painting and writing on silk, by the great calligrapher of the 4th century AD, Zhao Mengfu. The black script (above) is the most common form of writing in China today.

Writing in China

The first evidence of writing in China dates to the Shang dynasty of the middle of the second millennium BC. Unlike cuneiform and hieroglyphics, which gradually disappeared and were replaced by alphabetic scripts, Chinese writing has not changed drastically; the ancient script is similar to the present one.

The Chinese wrote with brush and ink on bamboo strips, silk cloth and bone. They also engraved inscriptions on bronze vessels. The earliest writings which have survived relate to divinations – questions asked of ancestors. The ancestors were contacted through oracle bones: animal shoulder blades or turtle shells were heated to produce cracks and then 'read'. The whole process was then recorded on the bone. Oracle bones have been a vital source of information about the Shang civilization.

▽ A letter written in ink on thin sheets of wood, one of over 200 found at the Roman fort of Vindolanda in England. Claudia Severa invites her friend Lepidina to her birthday party: 'On the third day before the Ides of September . . . I give you a warm invitation . . . to make the day more enjoyable for me by your arrival.

THE CLAY POTS SPEAK

Pottery was invented more than 10,000 years ago and was widely used by 2000 years ago. Although it breaks easily, it rarely disintegrates or dissolves. As a result fragments of pottery, called sherds, are the most common find on many archaeological sites. While such broken pieces often seem uninteresting, they hold a wealth of detailed information for the archaeologist to decipher.

Pottery was first used when groups began to settle permanently in an area. Pots were easy and cheap to make and could be used for many everyday purposes, including cooking and storage and transport of supplies. A range of other pottery objects were made, such as figurines, musical instruments, beads and implements used for hunting and fishing.

Archaeologists who specialize in studying pottery are called ceramic analysts (ceramic is another name for pottery). They can discover much about how pots were manufactured, and about how they were used and traded.

Making pots

Pots can be made by hand, with a potter's wheel or using a mould. In the past some families made their own pots, local potters made vessels for the village community, and large pottery workshops or factories

◁ Traditional pottery kiln in Tunisia. A clay kiln is built over stacks of unfired pots. The fire is set beneath them, with two holes at the bottom to provide a draught. Sometimes waste pots and pottery fragments are packed around the kiln to prevent hot gases escaping.

△ Potter in present-day Tunisia using a potter's wheel. There are three main ways of making pottery from clay: hand forming, mould forming and wheel forming. The most common, traditional way to produce large numbers of pottery vessels is on a potter's wheel.

produced pots in bulk for widespread distribution. Such activities still continue in many parts of the world today, and archaeologists can learn much from modern potters about traditional methods of pottery manufacture.

Pottery is made from clay which is then hardened by being heated (a process known as firing). Clay comes from the earth but the mineral composition of natural clay differs slightly from area to area. Microscopic analysis of minerals in clays can pinpoint their exact source. In this way we can tell how far the potter went in search of clay. Analysis can also show what substance the potter added to the clay (called temper) to harden it. This could be grit, sand, ground shell, straw, ground pottery fragments, blood or feathers; the more finely ground the temper, the better the pot.

Many kilns (used to fire pottery) have been found. However, some potters used open fires, which are more difficult to detect. Special techniques are used to determine the temperature at which a vessel was fired and whether it was fired in an open or closed kiln.

As the ceramic analyst can reconstruct how pots were made, it is possible to see if manufacturing techniques differed from region to region and so to detect local variations or styles.

WHAT WERE VESSELS USED FOR?

The shapes of pots may give us clues to their function. Pots with narrow, funnel-like openings, for example, would have been needed to prevent water or other liquids from spilling. Vessels with wider openings might have been used for storage. Many shapes could have served the same function. If a particular shape occurs often on a site, it might be simply because the potter or the group liked it.

Microscopic analysis of food residues in pots may reveal what people ate and drank and how they cooked their food. Residues of olive oil, butter, milk, cheese, wine and beer have been detected on pieces of pottery. Sometimes cooking vessels have a blackened exterior, which shows they were used over a fire.

Pottery is often found in burials or tombs. Cremated remains were usually placed in a pottery container and buried, sometimes accompanied by other artefacts. Pots containing offerings for the dead or to the gods are often found, for example in Egyptian tombs.

△ A vessel called a 'krater' from the Minoan civilization used for ritual ceremonies. Found at the Palace of Phaistos, Crete, it dates to between 2000 and 1700 BC.

▷ A pithos, one of the many huge jars in which grain and olive oil were stored in the Minoan Palace of Mallia on Crete.

TRADE AND CONTACT

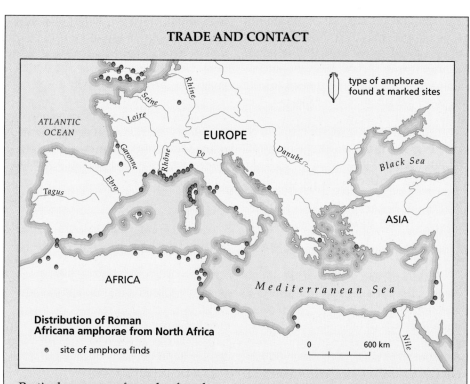

EUROPE

Rhine

Seine

Loire

ATLANTIC
OCEAN

Garonne

Rhône

Po

Danube

Black Sea

Ebro

Tagus

ASIA

AFRICA

Mediterranean Sea

Nile

type of amphorae
found at marked sites

**Distribution of Roman
Africana amphorae from North Africa**

● site of amphora finds

0   600 km

Particular groups of people often decorated pottery vessels with distinctive designs. We can therefore distinguish different groups within an area and determine where a pot originated. Some potters marked their pots with their name or an identification stamp. By marking the locations where these special pots were found, we can trace ancient trade routes and contacts between groups. The Mycenaeans of ancient Greece produced finely made pottery with distinctive designs which has been found throughout the

△ This particular type of amphora (storage jar), made in Roman North Africa, was used to store and transport olive oil.

Mediterranean region. They traded wine and olive oil in return for copper, ivory, tin, gold and alabaster.

Designs on pottery and vessel shapes tend to change slightly over time. It is therefore possible to place them in chronological order by looking at the different shapes or designs. In this way we can get relative dates for the pots (see page 24).

△ Moche portrait vessels with distinctive facial features represent individual people, most likely Moche chieftains. This one is wearing face paint and disc earrings. Moche pots and spouts were often made in separate moulds and then joined.

THE MOCHE POTTERS

Between 100 BC and AD 800 Moche chiefs ruled many thousands of people along a 400 km stretch of the northern coast of Peru. Most people lived in small fishing and farming settlements along the coast or in nearby river valleys. Others lived in towns. The largest towns had enormous pyramids and palace buildings made of sun-dried brick. These were used by the ruling classes, priests and their attendants.

The Moche had no written language but they were master craftspeople who vividly portrayed their life in pottery, metalwork and textiles. They were among the best potters in the world, producing

spectactular works of art. Their pots are so prized that unfortunately many Moche sites have been looted by robbers in search of pots to sell on the black market (illegally).

▷ A Moche shaman (medicine man) wearing a feline head-dress and disc earrings. He is performing a ritual, either curing a sick person or praying over a dead person.

Sculptures in clay

Moche pots reflect many different aspects of Moche life. They show rulers, priests, warriors, gods and ordinary people. They also depict plants, animals, hunting and fishing, and a host of other subjects.

Sometimes scenes were painted on the pots, but often the pots themselves were fashioned into particular forms. Important people had their portraits modelled in clay. These portrait pots bring to life the proud Moche rulers as vividly as any modern photograph.

Warriors must have been important in Moche society. They are often depicted wearing shirts and kilts decorated with pieces of metal or shells. At times their armour seems to be made of canes. Some warriors wear conical helmets, carry large clubs and look fearsome.

Prisoners taken in battle had an unhappy fate: stripped of weapons and clothes and tied to each other with ropes around their necks, they were marched back to the pyramid or temple where they were ritually executed.

The Moche potters did not forget the ordinary people. There are pots shaped in all sorts of realistic forms: men, women, women giving birth, women carrying babies on their backs, lovers, old people, musicians and messengers. We also see the blind, sick, diseased and deformed, as well as medicine men or curers. Nor are the dead forgotten: they appear in skeleton form, with clearly depicted expressions of pleasure, pain, terror or peace on their faces.

Artists also painted scenes of everyday life on the pots; these are a vital aid in reconstructing Moche life. Textiles were important but few have been preserved. However, scenes show women weaving using a loom similar to those used in parts of South America today.

Plants and animals in Moche life

A detailed list of the animals in the Moche environment can be compiled from looking at the pottery. As well as pots shaped as birds, frogs and lizards, there were deer, llamas, jaguars, pumas and a variety of fish and shellfish.

The pots also tell us how the Moche people hunted and fished. Men used clubs to drive deer into nets and then killed them with spears. They hunted birds with blowguns and killed seals with clubs. They fished from reed boats similar to those seen in the area today. Sometimes they caught fish in large nets.

Plants, too, are well documented. Indeed, archaeologists have used pottery as their main source of information on the food plants used by the Moche: maize (corn), beans, peanuts, potatoes, peppers, squash, gourds, cacti and a variety of fruits.

▷ Moche stirrup pot (named so because of the spout) with the body of a serpent and the head of a deer baring its feline fangs.

◁ This Moche vessel in the form of corn cobs with fantastic, human-like heads was probably used only during ritual ceremonies.

Moche beliefs

From the pottery we know that the sky god was the most important of the Moche gods. Many pots are formed in fantastic shapes or show unrealistic scenes. Some creatures are part animal and part human, warriors have wings and beaks, animals have human headdresses. These pots would have had a special meaning for the Moche people, although we do not know what it was.

Christopher Donnan, an American specialist in Moche art, has spent many years studying Moche pottery. According to him, the Moche had plain pottery for daily use and decorated pottery for special purposes. The important part that religion and a belief in supernatural forces must have played in Moche life is reflected in their superb pottery.

Although we may never unravel all the secrets of these ancient people, the pots reveal a wealth of information about Moche life.

BURYING THE DEAD

Graves are the final resting places for the physical remains of men, women and children. Careful excavation often reveals much about the dead people themselves and the society in which they once lived.

People show care and respect for the dead by burying them according to the customs of the society in which they live. For many people burial has a religious meaning tied to a belief in life after death. We are not sure when deliberate burial of the dead began but we know it is an ancient tradition. More than 40,000 years ago a Neanderthal group carefully buried a man, two women and a child inside Shanidar Cave in northern Iraq. Pollen analysis of the earth around the man's body has led some people to claim that it had been covered with flowers.

About 23,000 years ago a boy, a girl and a man were buried at Sungir, which is 200 km from Moscow. Stone artefacts, spears and carvings made from mammoth ivory were deliberately placed with the bodies. The man's cap was decorated with perforated fox teeth. Thousands of ivory beads were found on and around the bodies; these had been used to decorate the clothes, which have long since disintegrated. It has been estimated that it would have taken a person about 45 minutes to make each bead.

Bodies can be buried (called inhumation) or cremated. They may be treated in a special way such as mummification (preservation in special ointments) or perhaps placed in a particular position (curled up or straight) or facing in a specific direction. Objects (known as grave goods) sometimes accompany burials; these must have had special significance for the dead person and for those who conducted the burial.

The way people are buried and the grave goods buried with them may indicate their importance or status in the community. Societies have different traditions, however. Archaeologists sometimes assume that a rich tomb indicates a person of power and that simple graves with few or no grave goods belong to ordinary people. However, in some societies rich and powerful people may have been buried quite simply. Objects which are considered to be of value and show status may also vary from group to group.

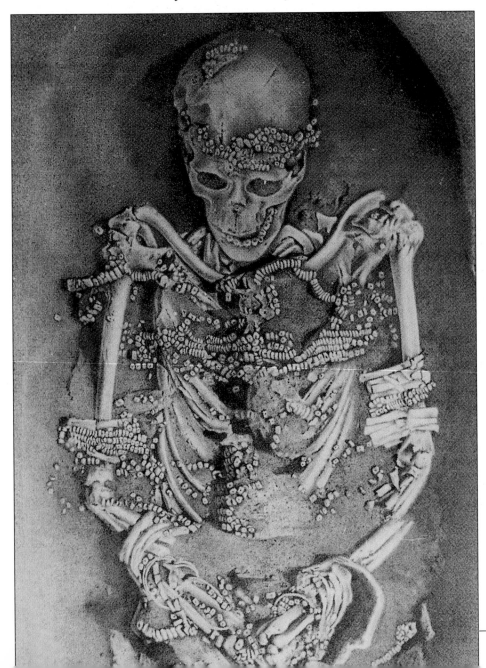

◁ This man and two children had been carefully buried in graves at Sungir in Russia about 23,000 years ago. Their bodies were decorated with more than 10,000 ivory beads and 200 fox teeth, which had holes drilled through them.

Is it right to excavate burials?

The decision to excavate graves requires careful consideration, as ancient peoples would probably not have wanted their loved ones to be disturbed. Although archaeologists wish to learn about past peoples, they have to decide whether it is really necessary to study graves and grave goods in order to do so. If they decide to excavate then they must always be aware of the special nature of the excavation. Many modern groups do not want archaeologists to interfere with the remains of their ancestors. Such is the case with Australian aborginal peoples and native American peoples in North America. In these cases excavation can be undertaken only with the consent and help of the modern descendants.

Evidence from the bodies

The bodies themselves may reveal much about the individual: their age, sex, height, cause of death, state of health during life, and diet. Bones often hold clues about the work people did when they were alive and any periods of illness or malnutrition they might have had.

They may also indicate particular diseases which might have affected a community. A study of more than 400 burials in the 3rd–5th century AD Romano-British cemetery in Cirencester in England is revealing. Study of the bones shows that many people had had problems with their backs and most had suffered from arthritis. Their work must have included pulling, pushing, lifting and carrying heavy loads. Signs of fractures were common, but most had healed naturally without the need for surgical treatment. Some arm and leg fractures may have occurred through tripping over or falling, but others (for example those

△ A six-month-old Inuit baby was buried with seven other people at Qilakitsoq, Greenland, about AD 1475. The bodies had been perfectly preserved by the cold conditions. Archaeologists were able to determine how old they were, and to learn about the clothes they wore, the food they ate, the diseases they suffered from, and their family relationships.

◁ Part of Tutankhamun's tomb as it was discovered in 1922. Unlike many other Egyptian tombs, it had not been looted. It was packed with rich grave goods and food to help the Pharaoh on his journey into the afterworld. Tutankhamun was not an important Pharaoh, and we can only guess at the riches of the tombs of the mighty Pharaohs.

affecting ribs) may have been the result of aggression. Sword or axe wounds, some lethal, showed that fighting – in battle, in the arena or in the town – occurred regularly. The dental evidence indicates that the people had a diet which was low in carbohydrates and sugary foods.

Relationships between people may also be detected from burials in cemeteries. For example, archaeologists studying the cemetery site of Mözs in Hungary (5th century AD) have been able to distinguish the burials of four separate families spanning three generations.

Corpses can also provide information about special practices that occurred during life in some societies, such as the distorting of heads and the filing or extraction of teeth. From burials, archaeologists know that the third generation at Mözs in Hungary practised head distortion. We also know that the ancient Maya of Mesoamerica often made holes in their teeth into which they inserted inlays of gold, jadeite or turquoise.

Evidence from the grave goods

Some of the most spectacular archaeological treasures have come from tombs. Howard Carter wrote that he was struck dumb on seeing the magnificence of the tomb of the young Egyptian Pharaoh Tutankhamun. When Lord Carnarvon, who subsidized the archaeological expedition, asked Carter what he had seen, Carter could only reply 'wonderful things'. Indeed the tomb was packed with gold, silver and bronze items, precious stones and a host of other dazzling objects – a tomb fit for a king.

We know from their writings that the Egyptians believed there was a life after death. They wanted to ensure that the dead person had all the necessary equipment to travel from this life into the next. As well as burying the young Pharaoh in a manner befitting his status, they also placed a supply of different types of food in the burial chamber to sustain him during his journey.

A royal Sumerian burial

Evidence of sumptuous burial is not confined to Egypt. Spectacular funeral practices have been documented worldwide and throughout time. Between 1922 and 1934 the Englishman Sir Leonard Woolley excavated 16 magnificent tombs at the cemetery of Ur in ancient Sumer (2600 BC).

As the cemetery contained many other tombs without grave goods archaeologists believe that the rich tombs must be those of the most important people in Sumerian society, perhaps royal personages (although we do not know if there were actually kings and queens in Sumer). The richness of these tombs rivalled that of Tutankhamun's tomb. But there was a macabre addition: they contained the bodies of royal followers and servants who had been sacrificed during the burial ceremony, presumably to accompany their royal master or mistress on the journey to the next life. Excavation of one royal grave

SUTTON HOO – AN ANGLO-SAXON CEMETERY

A group of mounds at Sutton Hoo in Suffolk can be traced on a map dated 1601. The first recorded excavations occurred in 1938. Since then two important excavations have been undertaken, the latest ending in 1992. The resulting evidence indicates that the mounds were part of an Anglo-Saxon cemetery in which the first kings of East Anglia, their comrades and relatives were buried.

Different burial practices have been documented at Sutton Hoo. The most spectacular are associated with ships – one in a chamber in a ship and one in a chamber under a ship. Inhumations in underground chambers and in coffins, and burials of cremated remains under mounds, have also been identified. Ritual

◁ The Standard of Ur, found with the royal burials at Ur. It is a box decorated with a mosaic of shell, red limestone and lapiz lazuli. The two long sides show the Sumerians at war and as victors. In the bottom two scenes on the war side the Sumerian infantry and charioteers kill the enemy and take captives. In the top scene, the king, who is taller than his men, inspects the war captives. Some captives are naked and some are wounded.

revealed 74 attendants, each with a small pottery cup, which Woolley suggests held the poison they may have drunk.

Burials in China

In China, too, the practice of ritual human sacrifice is seen in rich tombs of the Shang period more than 3200 years ago. The burial site at Anyang in north-east China contained more than 1000 small graves and eleven large tombs of Shang rulers. Buried with the rulers were the bodies of those who had been sacrificed and a mass of stone, jade, shell, bone, antler, pottery and bronze artefacts. It has been estimated that it would have taken 100 people 70 days to dig each large grave.

In later times sacrificed humans were replaced by lifesize replicas of people. In the 3rd century BC the first Chinese emperor, Qin Shi Huangdi, ordered thousands of terracotta (pottery) warriors to be made. He commanded that they should be buried next to his tomb when he died.

▷ In the early 3rd century BC Qin Shi Huangdi became the first emperor of China. He is buried under an immense burial mound near Xian City. He had an army of over 7000 soldiers, horses and chariots made in terracotta and buried in three pits near the tomb. The figures are all lifesize and dressed according to rank and battalion. Their uniforms were painted in bright colours, which have since faded. The soldiers' wooden spears and the leather harnesses of the horses have disintegrated. This huge army forms a tiny part of the burial complex.

▷ Reconstruction of a helmet from the Sutton Hoo ship burial from the pieces found during excavation. It was made of iron, bronze and garnets.

sacrifices of humans and animals, especially horses, have been associated with a few burials. While grave goods were found in all burials under mounds, some graves – perhaps those of the kings – were particularly rich in artefacts.

Burial in a ship

The ship burial under Mound 1 is the most famous at Sutton Hoo. A wooden chamber had been built in the middle of a 27 m-long rowing boat. The ship had been placed in a trench below the ground and covered with earth and sand to form a mound. Over the years the timber of the ship itself disintegrated: when the mound was excavated in 1939 only the metal rivets used to nail the timbers together remained. However, the shape of the ship was impressed in the hardened sand.

Patches of decayed wood found overlying the grave goods in the centre of the ship showed where the wooden burial chamber had been. The grave goods included everyday objects such as wooden buckets, wooden bottles and bronze cauldrons, as well as items of great value made of silver, gold, bronze, iron, semi-precious stones, rich cloth and leather.

Finding the body

The excavations in 1939 failed to reveal a body. At first archaeologists thought that the ship was a monument to a dead ruler whose body had been buried elsewhere. However, bodies can disintegrate in the acid soils of Sutton Hoo. As decay progresses the phosphate in the bodies seeps into the surrounding area. In 1967 specialists from the British Museum tested for phosphate. Higher levels found on certain grave goods indicated where the body had been. In other graves the missing skeleton was identified by a staining of the soil in the shape of the body. These have been called 'sand bodies'.

Was he a king?

Several lines of evidence indicate that the ship burial was that of a royal leader. The amount of gold and garnet jewellery and its superb craftsmanship suggest someone of importance. Some Anglo-Saxon graves have spears, but rarely more than one.

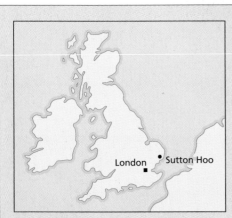

△ Location of the Sutton Hoo cemetery in East Anglia. Between the 6th and 8th centuries AD rulers of the East Anglian kingdom (possibly the Wuffinga dynasty) were buried here.

△ Excavating the Sutton Hoo boat in 1939. The lines of iron rivets which held the wooden frame together remain. The wood has disintegrated but the shape of the boat is impressed in the sand.

△ The richly decorated lid of a leather purse (long ago disintegrated) from Sutton Hoo. 40 gold coins were found under the lid; these may have been to pay for the dead person's voyage into the afterlife.

There were six spears in the ship burial. Other particularly fine artefacts include a richly decorated iron and bronze helmet, which is similar to chieftains' helmets from Sweden of the same period; a fine iron sword and a stone bar on to which a bronze stag fits, which some archaeologists suggest may be a sceptre – a sign of royal office. In addition, a huge trench had to be dug and the boat itself pulled from the nearby river and placed in it. It seems unlikely that so much effort would have been made for the burial of anyone less important than a royal leader.

Other graves at Sutton Hoo

Many more graves have been found since the 1939 excavation, especially during the excavations conducted by Professor Martin Carver between 1983 and 1992. He and his team undertook a systematic surface survey of the area and opened two large trenches crossing the site from north to south and east to west. They were then able to find the edges of the cemetery. They used sophisticated subsurface techniques to find archaeological areas and discovered two groups of sacrificial burials. Some of the bodies had their hands tied; others had been hanged or beheaded. There were no grave goods with these bodies. One group of bodies was near a burial mound while the second group was some distance away.

The burial of the Sutton Hoo prince

The grave of a young man was excavated in 1991. The rich grave goods indicated that this was a royal or aristocratic grave. The remains of a horse were found in a pit near the grave – possibly the young man's horse.

Carver was able to deduce the sequence of events in the burial ritual from the stratigraphy. It had rained after the pit had been dug. Later, grave goods were placed in the pit, leaving an empty area for the coffin. When the coffin was lowered into the grave, part of it settled on top of some grave goods. The grave was then covered with a 30 cm-deep layer of earth. A wooden bucket was next placed in the grave. Carver suggests that this was the horse's feeding bucket and the horse may have been killed at this time and buried with the young prince.

Dating the burials

Dates on the coins in the ship burial range between 575 and 625. The burial could not therefore have taken place before the date of the latest coin, 625. The styles of the grave goods in all the burials are similar to those of the 7th century, particularly the early part of the century. Carbon 14 techniques show that all the graves dated so far are from the 6th to 8th centuries AD, the time when the Anglo-Saxons became Christians.

Who were the Sutton Hoo kings?

We cannot be sure exactly who is buried at Sutton Hoo. However, we know from written history that the first kings of the Sutton Hoo area were from the Anglo-Saxon Wuffinga dynasty. Four kings ruled during the early 7th century: Raedwald, Sigeberht, Eorpwald and Ecric. Some or all of these may have had their final resting place in the Sutton Hoo cemetery.

▽ The burials of a young man, known as the Sutton Hoo prince, and his horse, excavated in 1991.

GLOSSARY

aboriginal people The original native people of a country.

absolute dating Methods used to determine the exact date (in years) of an artefact or site. Compare RELATIVE DATING.

aerial photography Detection of buried sites through photographs taken from the air.

amphitheatre An oval theatre used in Roman times for fights between gladiators and fights between wild and tame animals.

anaerobic environment An oxygen-free environment.

Anglo-Saxon Belonging to the period in England between about AD 400 and 1100.

anthropology The study of all aspects of humankind.

archaeobotany The study of plant remains from archaeological sites.

archaeozoology (faunal analysis) The study of animal bones from archaeological sites.

artefact Any object, which can be easily carried, that has been made, used or modified by humans, for example stone or metal tools, jewellery or pottery.

aurochs Wild cow or ox.

Australopithecus The earliest human ancestor with both apelike and human features.

barrow Mound of earth which usually covers a burial.

biface (hand axe) A pebble or flake of stone which has been worked on both sides to produce a regular shape and sharp edge.

biostratigraphy A relative dating method based on fossil animals or plants. Artefacts found in the same layer of deposits as a fossil plant or animal must be at least as old as the fossil.

blade A stone tool which has long, usually parallel edges.

Bronze Age The period, before the use of iron, when tools and weapons were usually made in bronze. It extends from about 2000 BC to about 300 BC, depending on the geographical region.

carbon 14 (C-14) A method of radioactive dating which is used to date all organic material – wood, charcoal, bones, plants and shells. It can be used to calculate the dates of objects up to 50,000 years old.

carnivore A meat-eating animal.

charred Blackened by fire.

classical archaeology The study of ancient Greece and Rome.

context The surrounding and exact location in which artefacts are found. This includes the type of deposit (for example soil or gravels) and any other artefacts nearby which may provide information about the finds.

core A cylindrical sample of soil or sediment collected from an area using a special tube-like instrument, also called a core.

core The original block or pebble of stone from which flakes have been removed in stone toolmaking.

cremation The burning of a dead body.

cuneiform A form of writing which left wedge-shaped marks in wet clay.

datum A clearly visible point on an archaeological site which is used as a fixed reference point for measuring the exact vertical and horizontal location of everything on the site.

deep sea core Core of sediments taken from the ocean bed which can show changes in temperature as far back as 2 to 3 million years ago and which is used in relative dating.

demotic A type of writing in ancient Egypt which developed about 600 BC. It was used for everyday purposes.

dendrochronology (tree ring dating) A method of absolute dating based on the annual growth rings of new wood on trees.

domesticated plants and animals Plants and animals which have been cultivated or bred by humans.

ecofact Plant and animal remains on an archaeological site.

environmental archaeology The study of plants and animals from archaeological sites in order to reconstruct past environments.

ethnoarchaeology The study of the way modern human groups live and the evidence left by their activities in order to help understand how archaeological sites may have been formed in the past.

ethnography The study of modern groups of aboriginal peoples, usually done by living with them, observing them and collecting information from them.

evolution The process by which all living things develop from simple to complex forms.

excavation The removal of earth from an archaeological site in a systematic manner in order to recover archaeological data.

experimental archaeology Experiments carried out by archaeologists to see how objects may have been made and how activities could have been carried out in the past.

faunal analysis *see* ARCHAEOZOOLOGY.

feature Evidence of human activities which cannot be moved. Hearths, post holes and rubbish pits are examples of features.

flake A piece of stone removed from a stone block or pebble during stone tool manufacture.

flint A rock which breaks in a regular pattern, which makes it good for making stone tools.

flint knapper A person who makes stone tools.

fossil The remains of plants, animals or humans preserved in rock.

garbage archaeology The study of modern garbage (rubbish) in order to learn about modern societies.

geology Study of how the earth was formed.

geomorphology The study of how landscapes formed and developed.

glyph A sign or symbol in a writing system.

grave goods Objects which are placed with a burial.

hammerstone A stone pebble used as a hammer to knock flakes off flint or other stone when making stone artefacts.

hand axe *see* BIFACE.

hearth A fireplace on an archaeological site.

herbivore An animal that eats only grass or plants.

hieratic A simplified, cursive (joined-up) form of Egyptian hieroglyphic writing.

hieroglyphic writing Writing using pictures. Hieroglyphic writing was first invented in Egypt about 3000 BC.

historic archaeology The study of those periods for which written documents as well as archaeological evidence are available.

hominid The zoological name given to humans and pre-humans.

Homo erectus Latin for 'upright man'. Lived between 1.6 and 0.5 million years ago.

Homo habilis Latin for 'handy man'. An early human ancestor in Africa between 2 and 1.5 million years ago.

Homo sapiens sapiens Latin for 'knowledgeable man'. The name given to modern humans.

horizontal excavation Uncovering a site by removing each layer separately over the whole site or a large area of a site. It gives a picture of the site at a particular time.

höyök *see* TELL.

Ice Age A period when glaciers covered much of the northern world.

in situ Archaeological remains which are found in almost exactly the same position as when they were originally left.

Indus civilization The first civilization in Pakistan and India, which developed along the Indus River.

industrial archaeology The study of the industrial remains of past societies.

inhumation The burial of a human body.

inorganic material Material which does not originate from plants or animals, for example rocks and metals.

Inuit The correct term for Eskimo.

Iron Age The period when iron replaced bronze for the manufacture of tools and weapons. It occurred between 1100 BC and the 19th century AD, depending on the region.

knapping The deliberate breaking of stone by humans to produce stone tools.

lintel The stone laid on top of and joining two upright stones.

lithic analysis The study of the manufacture and use of stone artefacts.

loess Fine silt dust from glaciers.

mammoth A huge, extinct species of elephant adapted to Ice Age conditions.

marrow The highly nutritious, fatty substance in the middle of bones.

Maya A Mesoamerican civilization, at the height of its power between AD 200 and 850.

megalith A large stone. Megalithic monuments constructed from large stones have been found throughout the world.

Mesoamerica The term used by archaeologists for the geographical region which includes Mexico, Guatemala, Costa Rica, Belize and Honduras.

Mesolithic The middle part of the Stone Age.

Mesopotamia Name of the ancient region between the Tigris and Euphrates Rivers and their tributaries and comprising modern-day Iraq and northern Syria.

metallurgical analysis The study of metal artefacts and waste products to discover how they were made and used and where the raw materials originated.

microwear analysis Examination of the edges of flint artefacts with microscopes to determine what the artefacts were used for and how they were used.

Middle Ages The period between about AD 500 and 1500.

millennium A period of 1000 years.

mortar A stone vessel in which substances, especially grain, are placed and then pounded or crushed with a pestle.

mosaic A pattern or picture made with small pieces of glass or stone or other material.

mummification The treatment of a dead body with special oils and spices so that it does not decay.

myth A story or tradition which often expresses popular beliefs about the world.

Neanderthal A group of human ancestors who lived in Europe and western Asia between about 100,000 and 33,000 years ago.

Neolithic (New Stone Age) The final part of the Stone Age. It was a period before metals were used, when farming first began to appear.

New Stone Age *see* NEOLITHIC.

nomad A member of a group that has no permanent home and regularly moves around from place to place.

obsidian The glassy stone produced by volcanoes which has a very sharp edge.

occupation level Area on an archaeological site which shows evidence of human occupation at one specific period of time.

ochre A red mineral which can be ground into powder, often used for decoration.

organic material Anything made of plants or animals, for example wood, charcoal, bones, plants and shells.

palaeogeography The study of the geography of ancient landscapes.

palaeography The study of ancient writing.

Palaeolithic (Old Stone Age) The period from the emergence of the first hominids to the end of the last Ice Age (4 million to 10,000 years ago).

palaeontology The study of fossil plants and animals.

pestle A tool, usually stone, used to pound or crush substances in a mortar.

polished stone axe A stone biface with a surface which has been made smooth by grinding and polishing with grit and water.

pollen analysis The study of fossil pollen grains in order to reconstruct past environments and detect changing climates.

potassium-argon (K-Ar) A method of radioactive dating which provides a date for the time of a volcanic eruption. It can be used to date volcanic rocks which are more than 100,000 years old.

potsherd (sherd) A fragment of pottery.

pottery Clay material which can be moulded when wet and soft and then hardened by heating (firing).

prehistoric archaeology The study of human development during the period before writing was known.

quern A large grinding stone used for grinding cereal grains.

radioactive dating A method of dating based on the decay or disappearance of certain naturally occurring radioactive elements in different types of materials.

refitting The fitting together of stone flakes to the block from which they were removed (the core) to discover how, and in which order, the artefacts were made.

relative dating Methods used to determine if an artefact or occupation level is older or younger than another without providing an exact age.

rescue archaeology *see* SALVAGE ARCHAEOLOGY.

ritual A ceremony which has special meaning for those who take part.

salvage archaeology (rescue archaeology) The study – or in some cases actual moving – of archaeological sites which may be destroyed by modern construction or development.

sarsen A hard sandstone rock from which the largest stones at Stonehenge are made.

sediments The earth and other materials that cover and surround archaeological sites.

sherd *see* POTSHERD.

sickle Curved pieces of wood or bone fitted with sharp pieces (small blades) of flint and used to harvest plants.

sieving Passing soil removed during excavation through a series of sieves to catch small artefacts and ecofacts which were missed by the excavator.

site formation processes All the natural and human processes which have played a part in the formation of an archaeological site.

sleeper A beam which supports rails on a railway track.

soil analysis Study of the composition and formation of soils in archaeological sites.

stela (plural stelae) A stone slab which usually has inscriptions carved on it.

step trench A sloping series of steps used for excavating very deep sites.

steppe Vast area of grassland with few trees found near glaciers.

Stone Age The period before metals were used. The length of the Stone Age varies throughout the world as people began to use metals at different times. It is divided into three parts: the Palaeolithic (Old Stone Age), Mesolithic (Middle Stone Age) and Neolithic (New Stone Age).

stratigraphy Study of the separate layers, or strata, of deposits (for example soils, rocks, buildings) which accumulate over time. Under normal circumstances each layer is older than the one above it and younger than the one below.

stratum (plural: strata) A layer of deposits in an archaeological site. *see* STRATIGRAPHY.

subsurface detection Techniques used to detect buried objects and features.

survey Searching the landscape for signs of archaeological sites. This may be done by walking over the land surface, by aerial photography, or by using subsurface techniques.

tell (tepe, höyök) An artificial hill or mound. Over the centuries houses, often made of mudbricks, disintegrated and formed layer upon layer of collapsed dwellings. The term 'tell' is used in the Middle East, 'tepe' in Iran and 'höyök' in Turkey.

tepe *see* TELL.

terracotta The name given to baked clay.

test excavation (test pit) A small excavation, usually one metre square, undertaken in order to assess what lies beneath the ground.

thermoluminescence (TL) A method of radioactive dating which is used to date pottery and burnt flints. It provides the date when the pottery was fired or the flints burnt.

Three Age System A system which divides European prehistory into three successive periods according to the materials in which tools were made in each period: Stone Age, Bronze Age and Iron Age.

trench Excavation of a rectangular area of a site, rather like a narrow passage.

typology The classification of artefacts into groups or types which are similar in some way.

Upper Palaeolithic A period of the Ice Age between about 40,000 and 10,000 years ago.

vertical excavation Removal of deposits by excavating downwards through a part of an archaeological site.

Vikings People from Scandinavia between AD 700 and 1100.

INDEX

Where several page references are given for a particular headword, the more important ones are printed in bold (e.g. **41**). Page numbers in italic (e.g. *94*) refer to illustrations and captions.

ACKNOWLEDGEMENTS

Design: Julian Holland
Abbreviations: t = top; b = bottom; l = left; r = right; c = centre;
BM = British Museum, London

Photographs
The publishers would like to thank the following for permission to
reproduce the following photographs:

AA Photo Library: 115; 117t
Agence photographique de la réunion des Musée Nationaux, France: 139
  (Louvre)
AKG London: 76 (Erich Lessing); 92b (Erich Lessing); 120t (V&A); 130-1
Brian & Cherry Alexander: 124
Allsport UK Ltd: 79 (Bob Martin)
Ancient Art & Architecture Collection: 4tl; 39t; 59b; 68bl; 82t; 82-3; 84t, b;
  85b; 87b; 90b; 91b; 93; 104t; 142t
Ashmolean Museum, Oxford: 52-3
Bodleian Library, Oxford: 102b
Bridgeman Art Library: 4tr (University of Oslo); 141t (Smithsonian
  Institution, Washington, DC); *Giraudon/Bridgeman Art Library:* 106
  (Diego Rivera, National Palace, Mexico City)
British Museum: 14; 21t; 74-5t (Nina de Garin Davies); 74t, b; 77; 141b; 150b
Ian Burgum: 117b
Gaynor Chapman: 67b
Clwyd Archaeology Services: 116 (Clwyd County Council, Stephen
  Grenter)
Colorific Photo Library Inc: 53b (P. Essick-Aurora)
Comstock Photo Library: 16-17; 56
C M Dixon Photo Resources: 4b; 8t; 45; 64t; 80t; 81; 90t; 142r; 143l, r; 144t
Dorset County Museum: 12t
English Heritage Photographic Library: 5t; 57b; 58; 61
ET Archive: 86
Werner Forman Archive Ltd: 3 (BM); 9tr (Silkeborg Museum, Denmark);
  10; 22r (BM); 89; 92t; 102t (Liverpool Museum); 105b; 107 (BM);
  144b (Museum fur Volkerkunde, Berlin); 145t, b (Museum fur
  Volkerkunde, Berlin)
Sonia Halliday Photographs: 51 (Jane Taylor)
Robert Harding Picture Library: 5b; 22t (Paolo Koch); 57t (Adam Woolfit);
  59t (Adam Woolfit); 65 (Paolo Koch); 66-7; 72 (Adam Wolfitt, BM);
  73b (Robert Francis); 80b; 91t; 142l (Ghigo Roli); 146t
Kate Hartnell: 126t; 129
Michael Holford Photographs: 6-7; 9tl (BM); 22l; 23b; 25 (BM); 73t (BM);
  75b (BM); 83t (Collection Marquis Northampton, Castle Ashby); 85t;
  114b; 138t; 138b (BM); 140t, b (BM); 148-9 (BM); 150t (BM); 151t (BM)
Jim Holmes: 66
Illustrated London News: 147b
Images Colour Library Ltd: 55
Institute of Archaeology, University College, London: 11t (Ken Walton); 12b
  (Peter Drewett); 13t, bl, br (Ken Walton); 14tl (Gordon Hillman);
  15t (Warwick Bray); 16 (Ruth Whitehouse); 23t (Carl Phillips);
  50l, r (Peter Dorrell); 52tl, bl (Peter Dorrell); 136b (Ian Glover)
Institute of Human Origins, California: 17 (Nancy Kahn); 18 (Nancy
  Khan); 20b; 33 (W. H. Kimbel)

Alan D. Levenson: 126-7
MacQuitty International Photographic Collection: 64b (Karachi Museum);
  68tl, tr; 69t; 120-1t; 121t, b
Mary Rose Trust: 110; 111tl, b; 112t, b; 113t, b
O. Louis Mazzatenta: 87t (National Geographic Society)
Milepost 92½, Colin Garratt: 114t
Brian Morrison: 9br
National Museum of Greenland: 147t
Natural History Museum Picture Library: 8b; 32l, r; 132t; 133
Network Photographers: 62 (Mike Goldwater)
Novosti: 146b
Oxford Scientific Films Ltd: 46-7 (Rafi Ben-Shahar); 136-7 (Steve Turner)
Panos Pictures: 36t (John Miles); 122 (Penny Tweedie)
Parks Canada: 97 (Birgitta Wallace); 98t (B. Schouback); 98-9 (Birgitta
  Wallace); 99r (D. Crawford)
Photographers/Aspen, David Hiser: 101; 103; 104-5
Planet Earth Pictures: 108 (Flip Schulke)
Maria Angeles Querol: 19t
Zev Radovan: 48t, b; 49
Research Project Mohenjo Daro/RWTH Aachen: 63; 69b (Georg Helmes)
Science Photo Library Ltd: 19b (John Reader); 21b (Alexander Tsiaras); 26
  (A. Hart-Davis); 26-7 (J. King-Holmes); 30-1 (J. Reader); 34t
  (J. Reader); 34b
Southern Methodist University, Texas, Lewis Binford: 125
Stofnun Arna Magnússonar a Islandi Reykjavik: 95 (Johanna Oílasfsdottir)
Tony Stone Images: 54b (Joe Cornish)
Sygma: 132-3 (Jean Clottes, Ministère de la Culture)
Telegraph Colour Library: 1 (China Pictorial); 2 (Terrence Spencer); 15b
  (J. Shenai); 111tr (P. Armiger); 149; 120-1b (Terrence Spencer)
Tropix Photographic Library: 123 (J. Wollard)
UNESCO: 118 (Dominique Roger); 120b (Nenadovic)
University of Arizona, William Rathje: 127; 128
University of Indiana, Nick Toth: 37
University of Oxford, Derek Roe: 31b; 35
University of Paris, Claudine Karlin: 39b; 40; 41; 42t, b
University of the Witwatersrand, Johannesburg, Rock Art Research Unit: 137
  J. D. Lewis-Williams: 137
University of York, Sutton Hoo Research Project, Martin Carver: 151b
Jean Vertut: 134; 134-5; 135
York Archaeological Trust Picture Library: 20t
Zefa Pictures: 9bl (Goebel Kurt)

Cover
Front main photograph: Elizabeth Baquedano (Institute of Anthropology,
  Mexico City)
Front l, r: Michael Holford Photographs
Spine: Robert Harding Picture Library
Back cover: University of Oxford, MARE Project

Illustrations and diagrams
Richard Berridge, Specs Art Agency: 31

Lewis Binford: 125
Mike Codd: 78-9
Nick Hawken: 28
Richard Hook: 4–5; 38-9; 43; 70-1; 94-5; 100-1; 106
Oxford Illustrators: 44; 45; 128
Peter Sarson: 18; 24t, b; 26; 27; 33
Peter Visscher: 50-1; 56; 60; 60-1; 88; 109
All maps are by Olive Pearson

The publishers would also like to thank the following for supplying
reference material for artwork:

Kate Scott: 44, 45; Menson Bound: 109; Lewis Binford: 123; William
Rathje: 128

Written sources
The preparation of a book such as the *Young Oxford Book of Archaeology*
cannot be done without a great deal of research and background
reading. The author found most of her information in articles and
books by the following people:

F. Adouze, B. Allchin, R. Allchin, I. Andrews, P. Andrews, A. Ashmore,
A. P. Bahn, J. Baines, G. Bass, C. Batey, A. Behrensmeyer, E. Benson, L.
Binford, L. P. Bodu, F. Bordes, G. Bosinski, A. Bowman, W. Bray, D.
Brothwell, R. Buchanan, H. Bunn, A. Burl, A. Burton, M. Carver, R.
Castledon, J. Cerny, C. Chippendale, P. Connolly, T. Cornell, N.
Cossons, H. Crawford, R. Dale, R. David, S. Davis, J. Deetz, C. Donnan,
L. Drees, J. Enloe, R. Etienne, A. Evans, B. Fagan, B. W. Fairservis Jr, M.
Finley, P. FitzGerald, J. Flood, J. P. Geneste, I. Glover, J. Gowlett, J.
Graham-Campbell, S. Grenfer, J. Harris, R. Harris, K. Hudson, H.
Ingstad, G. Isaac, M. Jansen, G. Jean, D. Johanson, G. Jones, M. Julian, C.
Karlin, Z. Kaufulu, B. Kemp, K. Kenyon, R. Klein, E. Kroll, D. Lambert,
R. Layton, M. Leakey, R. Leakey, A. Leroi-Gourhan, R. Lewin, J. Lewis-
Williams, E. Mackay, J. Málek, E. Matos-Moctezuma, J. Matthews, J.
McIntosh, R. McNiesh, A. McWhirr, P. Mellars, J. P. Mohen, H.
Nissen, M. O'Kelly, J. Oates, G. Oegan, N. Olive, G. Pettinato,
S. Ploux, G. Posehl, N. Postgate, S. Rao, W. Rathje, H. Ray,
J. Reader, P. Rees, C. Renfrew, P. Rice, J. Richards, D. Roe, M. Rule, M.
Ruspoli, J. Sabloff, T. Säve-Söderberg, H. Schöbel, K. Shang,
R. Shearer, D. Smith, O. Soffer, M. Stead, A. Stine-Ingstad,
C. Stringer, J. Swaddling, N. Toth, B. Trinder, B. E. Twohig,
P. Vertut, M. Vickers, L. Viner, B. Wallace, C. Wells, Sir M. Wheeler, H.
Wilson, J. Wymer.

Consultants
The following people read and commented on different chapters in the
book and gave advice on illustrations:

P. Andrews, W. J. Blair, L. Blue, W. Bray, M. Carver, H. Crawford,
P. Drewett, A. Garrard, B. Ghaleb-Kirby, I. Glover, J. Graham-Campbell,
K. Hardy, A. Hildred, A. Johnston, J. Powell, P. Rice, D. Roe,
M. Roxan, J. Tate.